The Jacksonian Economy

THE NORTON ESSAYS IN AMERICAN HISTORY
Under the general editorship of
HAROLD M. HYMAN
William P. Hobby Professor of American History
Rice University

The Jacksonian Economy

Peter Temin

W · W · NORTON & COMPANY

New York · London

This research was supported by the National Science
Foundation and the Sloan Research Fund of the Massachusetts Institute of Technology. All responsibility for
views expressed herein is the author's

For Miguel Sidrauski
1939–1968

Contents

List of Tables and Figures

9

Preface

〰〰〰〰〰〰〰〰〰〰〰〰〰〰〰〰〰〰〰〰〰〰〰〰〰〰〰〰

THIS IS A BOOK about the interaction of economics and politics. Its purpose is to refute the commonly accepted view that Andrew Jackson's policies toward the Second Bank of the United States produced the dramatic boom and crises of the 1830's, a view that colors almost all modern evaluations of Jacksonian policies. The boom and crises were caused by events beyond the control of Andrew Jackson, and neither Jackson nor his followers deserve to be blamed for them. The Bank War has been analyzed often as a political phenomenon; its economic impact also needs to be correctly evaluated.

It is a great pleasure to acknowledge the contributions of those who have helped in the preparation of this book. Professors Stuart Bruchey, Robert L. Church, Richard S. Eckaus, Franklin M. Fisher, Duncan K. Foley, Frank O. Gatell, and Edward J. Kane read and criticized a part or draft of the argument. Donald Cimilluca and Lawrence Herron helped prepare the statistical tables. And the National Science Foundation and the Sloan Research Fund of the Massachusetts Institute of Technology helped to finance the research. I am grateful to these people and organizations for their help; any remaining errors are mine alone.

It is a great tragedy that the name of Miguel Sidrauski appears on the dedication page rather than among the people thanked here. This manuscript was on his desk at his untimely death, and it is undoubtedly poorer—as is the entire field of monetary economics—for the absence of his views. In tribute to the qualities that made Miguel Sidrauski a good friend and a fine economist, this book is respectfully dedicated to his memory.

The Jacksonian Economy

1

Introduction

THE HISTORIOGRAPHY of the Jacksonian period presents at least one curiosity to the modern observer. The period is noted both for great political changes and dramatic economic fluctuations. Yet while controversy continues to rage about the former, there appears to be an accepted interpretation of the latter that is agreed upon by all major authorities.

According to this interpretation, the economic fluctuations of the 1830's and early 1840's were the direct result of Andrew Jackson's political actions. By vetoing the recharter of the Second Bank of the United States in 1832 and removing the public deposits from the Bank in 1833, Jackson initiated an unsound credit expansion and inflation characterized by unprecedented speculation in public lands. The excesses of this boom would have produced a crisis in any case, but Jackson precipitated the Panic of 1837 by his policies toward the public land sales which had intensified the expansion and produced a surplus in the hands of the Federal Government. Jackson's Specie Circular of 1836 was designed to curb the sales, and the distribution of the surplus in 1837 was an attempt to dispose of the revenue already collected from them. Together they produced the Panic of 1837. After the panic the boom collapsed, and the economy slipped into one of the worst depressions it has known.

This story is clear, logical, and unambiguous. It shows unequivocally how Jackson's political program led the economy step by step to disaster. For those who do not admire Jackson, it has provided ample reason for rejecting his policies. For those

who support Jackson, it has represented the dire consequences
of good intentions thwarted by the speculative propensities of
the American people. In either case, the conviction that Jackson's policies were highly destructive of economic stability is a
major starting point for the evaluation of Jacksonian democracy.

Thus Arthur M. Schlesinger, Jr., said, "Above all, the Bank
War triumphantly established Jackson in the confidence of the
people," but admitted that, "In destroying the Bank, Jackson
had removed a valuable brake on credit expansion; and in spon-
soring the system of deposit in state banks, he had accelerated
the tendencies toward inflation." Richard Hofstadter agreed:
"In killing the bank he [Jackson] had strangled a potential
threat to democratic government, but at an unnecessarily high
cost." Marvin Meyers also concurred: "[T]he bank-boom-bust
sequence was the primal experience of Jacksonian life, which
fixed the content, tone, and terms of politics for as long as
Jacksonianism counted in America." And Bray Hammond
asserted, "Although the Bank was by no means the only thing
that occupied the Jacksonians, its destruction was apparently
esteemed by many of them their finest accomplishment," even
though, "over-trading, inflation, and speculation, . . . which
Andrew Jackson aimlessly deplored, could not have been more
effectively promoted by Jacksonian policies had that been their
purpose." [1]

Despite its universal acceptance, this story will not stand
close scrutiny; it is negated by the extant data of the 1830's.
Jackson's economic policies were not the most enlightened the
country has ever seen, but they were by no means disastrous.
The inflation and crises of the 1830's had their origin in events
largely beyond Jackson's control and probably would have

1. Arthur M. Schlesinger, Jr., *The Age of Jackson* (Boston: Little,
Brown, 1945), pp. 115, 218; Richard Hofstadter, *The American Political
Tradition* (New York: Knopf, 1948), p. 63 (page reference from the
Vintage edition); Marvin Meyers, *The Jacksonian Persuasion* (Stanford:
Stanford University Press, 1960), p. 103; Bray Hammond, *Banks and
Politics in America, from the Revolution to the Civil War* (Princeton:
Princeton University Press, 1957), pp. 361, 453.

taken place whether or not he had acted as he did. The economy was not the victim of Jacksonian politics; Jackson's policies were the victims of economic fluctuations.

The demonstration of this fact is straightforward. As Albert Gallatin noted at the time: "[T]he charges against the President for having interfered in the currency resolve themselves into the single fact of having prevented the renewal of the charter of the Bank of the United States." [2] As a result, so the story goes, banks expanded their notes and deposits without a corresponding increase in their specie reserves, that is, without just cause. Yet the actual sequence was that bank *reserves* increased rapidly in the 1830's and that banks did not increase the volume of their obligations faster than they received new reserves.[3]

This finding shatters the traditional interpretation of the 1830's. And as is usual with such findings, it raises more questions than it answers. If Jackson's destruction of the Second Bank did not cause the inflation, what did? And even if Jackson's actions in 1832 and 1833 did not start the boom, did his actions in 1836 stop it? How important was the Bank of the United States, and the political storm it aroused, to the economy? Has Jackson been blamed for economic fluctuations that he did not cause? The following pages will attempt to answer these questions, but a closer look at the traditional story will expose the questions that need answering more precisely.

The Traditional History of the Jacksonian Boom

The traditional story appears in one version or another in almost all the standard secondary works on the Jacksonian pe-

2. Albert Gallatin, *Suggestions on the Banks and Currency of the Several States, in Reference Principally to the Suspension of Specie Payments* (New York, 1841), p. 31.
3. The data are presented in Table 3.3, p. 71 and the sources are detailed in the Appendix. Bank notes and deposits were current obligations of banks. In other words, banks promised to pay gold or silver coins on demand for their notes and for checks drawn against their deposits. Gold and silver coins were referred to collectively as "specie," and banks had to keep reserves of specie in order to be able to pay it for their notes or for checks drawn on their deposits.

riod. Some versions are more complete than others, and none is definitive, but they are clearly all variations on a single theme. Before presenting a new version of the Jacksonian boom, it is useful to review the traditional account and the methods by which it was derived.

To show the emotional content of this history and the agreement among the sources, a canonical account has been compiled from the standard secondary sources. Despite occasional differences of emphasis, the concentration of all authors on the role of Jackson and the excessive nature of the banking expansion will be evident. Here, then, is the traditional history of the boom in the words of Hammond, Hofstadter, Meyers, Schlesinger, *et al.*

The story opens with the famous "Bank War" between Andrew Jackson, President of the United States, and Nicholas Biddle, president of the Second Bank of the United States. The most dramatic act of the "war," which ended in the "destruction" of the Second Bank, was Jackson's veto of the bill to recharter the Bank in 1832. "The message accompanying the veto is a famous state paper. It is legalistic, demagogic, and full of sham. Its economic reasoning was said by Professor Catterall, over 50 years ago, to be beneath contempt. Its level is now no higher." [4]

"Pursuing the bank war to its conclusion, Jackson found defeat in victory. Re-elected overwhelmingly on the bank issue in 1832, he soon removed all United States funds from the bank. . . . The federal deposits that Jackson had taken from Biddle were made available to several dozen state banks; these promptly used their new resources to start a credit boom." [5] "The proportion of paper to specie lengthened, gambling in banks, internal improvements and public lands grew more frenzied, and the economic structure became increasingly speculative and unsound." [6]

4. Hammond, p. 405. The reference is to Ralph C. H. Catterall, *The Second Bank of the United States* (Chicago: University of Chicago Press, 1902), p. 239.
5. Hofstadter, p. 63.
6. Schlesinger, p. 217.

"[E]verybody who could borrow money bought public land to sell again at the market value, or to hold for a further rise. In this way the deposits were borrowed, paid to the land receiver for land, to be by him deposited in the banks; then the operation was repeated again and again, the growing surplus consisting of bank credits mainly." [7] "Each bank could count the notes of other banks as reserves and expand its notes accordingly; with the general result that the more the banks lent the more they mutually augmented their reserves and the more they were able to lend. No legal requirements governed bank reserves before 1837 . . . and there was now no federal bank maintaining systematic pressure on the banks to redeem their notes." [8]

"It appears inevitable that the gaudy mid-thirties dream of sudden fortune should have collapsed. The credit inflation flowed from a highly vulnerable banking system lacking resources and techniques to sustain its commitments. The land bubble was balanced precariously upon a shaky credit structure, and had to fail as soon as a hard reckoning of values was enforced. The bond issues of the states created large immediate obligations against doubtful, sometimes hopeless, revenue prospects; a process of liquidation could not long be avoided. Briefly, the very excesses of the boom, inherently unstable, defined the necessity for a crisis as soon as faith faltered and bets were called." [9]

"Into this unstable situation, the federal government introduced several measures which aggravated the instability. First, Collectors of the Public Revenue were ordered not to receive small bank notes. Second, it was stipulated that on and after August 15, 1836 [,] public lands must be paid for with gold and silver. . . . This policy had the effect of attracting specie away from banks in the centers of commerce into outlying areas, such as Michigan, where land sales were large. Third, Congress au-

7. Edward G. Bourne, *History of the Surplus Revenue of 1837* (New York, 1885), pp. 14–15.
8. Hammond, pp. 452–53.
9. Meyers, p. 114.

thorized that the surplus in the Treasury above $5,000,000 be distributed to the states in proportion to their population. The distribution was to be made in quarterly installments beginning January 1, 1837." [10]

"Each quarterly installment, in consequence, was to be $9,367,215. Some of this money was in banks situated in the states to which it was to be distributed. Much was not. Some banks had enough cash and collectible loans to enable them to make their payments. Many had not. Over the country as a whole, the banks that had received the surplus were not in general the banks that held the gold and silver in which the surplus was to be distributed, and the funds in the individual states did not match the amounts to be distributed to those states. The requirements of the specie circular [that is, the second measure mentioned in the previous paragraph], aggravated by the distribution, produced absurd disorder." [11]

The federal charter of the Bank of the United States had expired in 1836, but the Bank had not ceased its operations. It had acquired a new charter from the state of Pennsylvania and was active in subsequent events. In fact, it was so active that most accounts of these years are concentrated on the Bank's actions. The Bank suspended specie payments in 1837, resumed them in 1838, suspended them again in 1839, and failed in 1841. Many banks followed suit, and the economy is reported to have had a crisis in 1837, renewed its prosperity in 1838, experienced a new crisis in 1839, and plunged into a severe depression in the early 1840's.[12]

The failure of the Bank of the United States has been analyzed in detail, but the reasons why the economy should have

10. Walter Buckingham Smith, *Economic Aspects of the Second Bank of the United States* (Cambridge: Harvard University Press, 1953), p. 185.
    11. Hammond, p. 456.
    12. Smith, Chap. 11; Hammond, pp. 467–90, 502–18; Douglass C. North, in *Growth and Welfare in the American Past* (Englewood Cliffs: Prentice-Hall, 1966), p. 32, said: "Probably the depression of 1839 [to 1843] was the most severe of the century."

been depressed are less clear. "Many factors contributed to the gravity of the slump. Most important undoubtedly was the violence and speculative nature of the boom that had preceded it. Public land sales had reached in 1836 a level which was never again to be equalled. The renewed suspension of the B. U. S. in 1839, following as it did on the widespread bank failures of 1837, caused a profound public mistrust of banks and bank credit generally. The failure on the part of nine of the states to pay the interest due on their debts destroyed American credit in Europe and made it out of the question for any more loans to be obtained in that way. And the state of the cotton market in Britain after 1840 could scarcely have been less hopeful." [13]

This is the traditional story. It is presented with remarkably little variation in any number of places.[14] The precise cause of

13. R. C. O. Matthews, *A Study in Trade-Cycle History: Economic Fluctuations in Great Britain, 1833–1842* (Cambridge, England: Cambridge University Press, 1954), p. 68.

14. This account, or references to it, appears in the following political and biographical studies: Carl Brent Swisher, *Roger B. Taney* (New York: Macmillan, 1935), pp. 331–33; Charles M. Wiltse, *John C. Calhoun, Nullifier, 1829–39* (Indianapolis: Bobbs-Merrill, 1949), pp. 287–88, 345–46; William Nisbet Chambers, *Old Bullion Benton, Senator from the New West* (Boston: Little, Brown, 1956), p. 222; Thomas Payne Govan, *Nicholas Biddle: Nationalist and Public Banker, 1786–1844* (Chicago: University of Chicago Press, 1959), pp. 301–02; Glyndon G. Van Deusen, *The Jacksonian Era: 1828–1848* (New York: Harper & Row, 1959), pp. 105–06; Walter Hugins, *Jacksonian Democracy and the Working Class* (Stanford: Stanford University Press, 1960), pp. 45, 178–79.

It also appears in the following economic studies: William Graham Sumner, *A History of Banking in the United States* (New York, 1896), pp. 230–32; Reginald Charles McGrane, *The Panic of 1837* (Chicago: University of Chicago Press, 1924), pp. 91–94; Oscar and Mary Flug Handlin, *Commonwealth; A Study of the Role of Government in the American Economy: Massachusetts, 1774–1861* (New York: New York University Press, 1947), p. 179; George Rogers Taylor, *The Transportation Revolution* (New York: Holt, Rinehart and Winston, 1951), pp. 340–42.

Additional economic history texts using this story are cited in J. R. T. Hughes and Nathan Rosenberg, "The United States Business Cycle Before 1860: Some Problems of Interpretation," *Economic History Review,* Second Series, XV (1963), 476–93.

It has found its way into standard texts, such as: Samuel Eliot

the crisis of 1837 is the only subject still in dispute, although the actions of President Jackson figure strongly in most explanations. Historians who say that the boom made a crisis inevitable place the responsibility for the crisis on Jackson's actions initiating the boom. Those who say that the Specie Circular, the distribution of the surplus, or both caused the crisis, also blame Jackson. But a few, who say that the Bank of England produced the crisis, dissent from this view.[15]

A New Approach

This account is in error at three main points. First, the boom did not have its origins in the Bank War. It resulted from a combination of large capital imports from England and a change in the Chinese desire for silver which together produced a rapid increase in the quantity of silver in the United States. Banks did not expand their operations because they were treating the government deposits as reserves, to finance speculation, or because the Bank of the United States was no longer restraining them; they expanded because their true—that is, specie—

Morison and Henry Steele Commager, *The Growth of the American Republic,* Fifth Edition (New York: Oxford University Press, 1962), I, 484–87; T. H. Williams, R. N. Current, and F. Freidel, *A History of the United States* (New York: Knopf, 1959), I, 385–88; Frank Thistlethwaithe, *The Great Experiment* (Cambridge, England: Cambridge University Press, 1955), p. 143.

Some authors writing about this period, however, do not even mention the boom or the causes of the Panic of 1837. See, for example, Carl Russell Fish, *The Rise of the Common Man, 1830–1850,* Vol. VI of Arthur M. Schlesinger and Dixon Ryan Fix (eds.), *A History of American Life* (New York: Macmillan, 1927); Lee Benson, *The Concept of Jacksonian Democracy* (Princeton: Princeton University Press, 1961); and Richard P. McCormick, *The Second American Party System: Party Formation in the Jacksonian Era* (Chapel Hill: University of North Carolina Press, 1966).

15. Ralph W. Hidy, *The House of Baring in American Trade and Finance* (Cambridge: Harvard University Press, 1949), p. 207. It is common for historians to note the actions of the Bank of England and even to assert their importance while at the same time continuing to blame Jackson for the crisis. See Hammond, p. 457, for example.

reserves had risen.[16] Second, the Panic of 1837 was not caused by President Jackson's actions. The "destruction" of the Bank of the United States did not produce the crisis because it did not produce the boom. The Specie Circular and the distribution of the surplus also did not have the effects attributed to them. And third, the depression of the early 1840's was neither as serious as historians assume nor the fault of Nicholas Biddle. It was primarily a deflation, as opposed to a decline in production, and it was produced by events over which Biddle had little control.

These errors have arisen because of the nature of the sources used to compile the traditional account. The most important source, as is usual in historical investigations, has been the opinion of informed contemporaries. There is no doubt that we must rely on the opinions of informed witnesses for an understanding of some aspects of the 1830's, but there is good reason to doubt that we can discover the whole story from their words. Most of these observers were also participants, and their objectivity may be questioned. Nicholas Biddle could not possibly have given a balanced account of Jackson's involvement with the Panic of 1837. Other contemporary observers held ideas about the operation of the economy that we can no longer accept today. Albert Gallatin, for example, former Secretary of the Treasury and dean of the New York banking community, could assert with great finality: "It has always been the opinion of the writer of this essay that a public debt was always an evil to be avoided whenever practicable; hardly ever justifiable ex-

16. Macesich noted that the reserves of the banking system had risen rapidly during the boom. This observation is correct, but Macesich's attempts to formulate a new interpretation of the boom were not entirely successful and have not been widely accepted. See George Macesich, "Sources of Monetary Disturbances in the U. S., 1834–1845," *Journal of Economic History,* XX (September, 1960), 407–34, and "International Trade and United States Economic Development Revisited," *Journal of Economic History,* XXI (September, 1961), pp. 384–85; Jeffrey G. Williamson, "International Trade and United States Economic Development: 1827–1843," *Journal of Economic History,* XXI (September, 1961), 372–83; Douglass C. North, *The Economic Growth of the United States, 1790–1860* (New York: Norton, 1966). pp. 198–202; and Chapter 3, below.

cept in time of war." [17] And even if the difficulties of personal subjectivity did not exist, the opinions of illustrious contemporaries would still not be a good source. They simply were not sufficiently consistent to provide the raw material for a unified account.

The two opinions most oft 'n quoted are those of Nicholas Biddle expressed in an open letter to John Quincy Adams, November 11, 1836, and the 1841 essay of Albert Gallatin from which an opinion was just quoted. Biddle supported one line of argument found in the traditional account by saying: "In my judgment, the main cause of it [the current crisis] is the mismanagement of the revenue—mismanagement in two respects: the mode of executing the distribution law, and the order requiring specie for the public lands." And Gallatin supported a different part of the story by announcing: "Overtrading has been the primary cause of the present crisis in America." [18]

Unfortunately, Biddle did not think much of the opinion expressed by Gallatin, and Gallatin did not agree with Biddle. Biddle noted in his letter that "it is said that the country has overtraded—that the banks have overissued, and that the purchasers of public lands have been very extravagant. I am not struck by the truth or propriety of these complaints. The phrase of overtrading is very convenient but not very intelligible. If it means anything, it means that our dealings with other countries have brought us in debt to those countries. In that case the exchange turns against our country, and is rectified by an exportation of specie or stocks in the first instance—and then by reducing [the ratio of] the imports to the exports. Now the fact is, that at this moment [November, 1836], the exchanges are all in favor of this country—that is, you can buy a bill of exchange

17. Gallatin, pp. 28–29.
18. Nicholas Biddle to J. Q. Adams, Nov. 11, 1836, reprinted in *Niles' Weekly Register,* LI (Baltimore, Dec. 17, 1836), 243–45; Gallatin, p. 26. See also the 1837 comments of Abbot Lawrence, in Hamilton A. Hill, *Memoir of Abbot Lawrence* (Cambridge, 1884), pp. 16–18. Hughes and Rosenberg document the use of the word "overtrading" and the prefix "over-" in the recent literature.

on a foreign country cheaper than you can send specie to that country." [19]

And as we have already noted, Gallatin said, "[T]he charges against the President for having interfered in the currency resolve themselves into the single fact of having prevented the renewal of the charter of the Bank of the United States." He went on to say, "The direct and immediate effects cannot be correctly ascertained; but they have been greatly exaggerated by party spirit. That he found the currency in a sound and left it in a deplorable state is true; but he cannot certainly be made responsible for the aberrations and misdeeds of the bank [of the United States] under either of its charters. The unforeseen, unexampled accumulation of the public revenue was one of the principal proximate causes of the disasters that ensued. It cannot be ascribed either to the President or to any branch of the government, and its effects might have been the same whether the public deposits were in the State banks, or had been left in the national bank, organized and governed as that was." [20]

These divergent views by well-qualified contemporary observers cannot be reconciled by appeals to opinion alone. Reference must be made to the actual events taking place. Such observations comprise the other main source of data for the traditional account, but they have not been used in any systematic fashion. Each author has chosen a few facts about the monetary system or the banking structure to present, but almost no one has tried to put these data into a systematic framework or tried to make explicit the implications of the cited observations.[21] As Brinley Thomas once said in a different context, the empirical data have been used "as a drunk uses lampposts: more for support than for illumination."

This can be seen clearly in the treatment of the core of the

19. *Niles'*, LI, 243–45.
20. Gallatin, pp. 31–32.
21. Exceptions to this rule are provided by Macesich, 1960, and Jeffrey G. Williamson, *American Growth and the Balance of Payments, 1820–1913: A Study of the Long Swing* (Chapel Hill: University of North Carolina Press, 1964).

traditional story of the boom: the nature of the "credit expansion." It is stated that banks used government deposits and notes of other banks as reserves, and that they expanded their activities without references to their true reserves, that is, specie. As Schlesinger phrased it in the passage just cited: "The proportion of paper [that is, bank obligations] to specie lengthened." Phrased another way, the reserve ratio of banks—the inverse of the ratio of obligations to specie—declined. But not one of the historians repeating this story cites any evidence on the reserve ratio of the banking system. One occasionally sees references to the behavior of individual banks and states, but never is there documentation of how the system as a whole behaved.

This gap in our knowledge of the 1830's has been extremely costly. The behavior of individual banks does not necessarily parallel the behavior of the banking system as a whole, and the experience of any single state is not always a good index of the progress of the Union. The story of the 1830's constructed from accounts of individual banks and states is seriously in error, and it can be corrected only by the use of data about the economy as a whole. Incorporated systematically into a coherent theoretical framework, the aggregate data on the 1830's enable us to discriminate between alternate hypotheses and schemes of causation. As a result, we can say both that the traditional account is invalid and that the alternate account to be presented here is supported at many points by the available data.

This demonstration is presented in the following pages. Although the investigation ends like any other historical inquiry with a narrative of events, it approaches the narrative from an unusual angle. The primary source materials are the data presented in the tables and the Appendix; they are numbers rather than words. In addition, most of the data are aggregate data. The data presented from time to time in contemporary journals such as *Niles' Weekly Register* concern isolated participants in the economy, and it is natural to try to generalize from their experiences. If data on the whole economy are available, however, they clearly provide a better index to the behavior of the whole economy than observations of a more restricted nature, and they are used here.

The account opens in Chapter 2 with an analysis of Jackson's veto of the Second Bank's recharter in 1832 and the message that accompanied it. This analysis provides an opportunity to explain the operations of the Second Bank and to make some judgments about the long-run impact of the veto. Chapter 3 provides an account of "Biddle's contraction" in 1834 and the subsequent boom. The data on specie flows and the money supply show clearly that the traditional explanation of the boom is incorrect, and the discussion is concerned with the formulation of an alternative. The expansion was followed by the Panic of 1837, and the various explanations that have been advanced for that crisis are examined in Chapter 4. The crisis was followed by fluctuations and a sharp deflation. These are described from the point of view of the economy as a whole in Chapter 5, demonstrating the comparatively minor role that the Bank of the United States played in them. Finally, the various threads of the story are drawn together in Chapter 6 to provide the basis for some conclusions about the antebellum economy and the relations between politics and economics.

2

Jackson's Veto of the Second Bank of the United States

THE TRADITIONAL STORY begins with President Jackson's veto of the recharter of the Second Bank of the United States. The recharter was proposed in 1832, although the Second Bank's existing charter was not due to expire until 1836. The recharter bill passed Congress and was vetoed by Jackson for reasons that have never been made entirely clear.[1]

One of the main sources of this confusion is the veto message itself. In this public document, Jackson set out some reasons for the veto. One would presume that at least the main lines of his objectives would be apparent in this document, but as Catterall and others have noted, the main appearance is of confusion.[2] Let us examine two of the contradictions in this message, looking not only at Jackson's reasoning, but at the actual operation of the economy. We shall regard the Second Bank as a dealer in exchange, as a source of capital, and as a central bank.

1. See Schlesinger; Hammond; Frank Otto Gatell, "Sober Second Thoughts on Van Buren, the Albany Regency, and the Wall Street Conspiracy," *Journal of American History,* LIII (June, 1966), 19–40; and Robert V. Remini, *Andrew Jackson and the Bank War* (New York: Norton, 1967) for various views.
2. See Chapter 1.

The Nature of Exchange Operations

The veto message opened by labeling the Second Bank a monopoly: "It enjoys an exclusive privilege of banking under the authority of the General Government, a monopoly of its favor and support, and, as a necessary consequence, almost a monopoly of the foreign and domestic exchange." [3] The "exclusive privilege" was the Bank's Federal charter. It was the only bank chartered by the Federal Government (except for a few unimportant banks in the District of Columbia), but states could and did charter banks also. The "monopoly of . . . favor and support" consisted in being the sole fiscal agent of the Federal Government. And, as Jackson said, the fiscal agent of the government dominated the exchanges; that is, the business of transferring money from place to place.

The tariff provided about 90 percent of the Federal Government's revenue.[4] This revenue was collected at the ports of entry to the country along the Eastern Seaboard. Federal expenditures were primarily for military ends, including the support of the Navy, interest on the public debt, and pensions for soldiers of the Revolutionary War. These expenses had a different geographic pattern from the revenues—although naval expenses were, like the revenues, concentrated at seaports—and the government's fiscal agent was the biggest dealer in the transfer of funds around the country. Part of the government's debt was held abroad, and its fiscal agent was a large dealer in international exchange as well. It would be untrue to say that the Second Bank had a monopoly in these areas, but it did dominate them.

The reasons for using a single fiscal agent are simple

3. Andrew Jackson, "Veto Message," July 10, 1832, in James D. Richardson, *Message and Papers of the Presidents, 1789–1897,* 10 vols. (Washington, 1898–99), II, 576–91.
4. Land sales rivaled the tariff as a source of revenue for a few years after the "bank war," but they normally raised only about one tenth the revenue derived from the tariff. See Table 5.3, page 168.

enough. The alternative was to use a variety of agents. Instead of a single bank with many branches, there would then be many banks in different places. Accordingly, the government would not be able to deal with a single agency which would allocate responsibility among the different branches; it would have to make these various administrative decisions itself. If the banks holding government deposits formed some kind of administrative agency to divide the responsibility among themselves, this would relieve the government of the extra trouble in dealing with many agents, but the administrative agency would differ in name only from being a sole fiscal agent.

Even when the government was willing to support the extra administrative expense necessary to deal with several fiscal agents in the 1830's, these banks had a "monopoly" of the government's business. The fact that there were several members of this favored group, not just one, did not hide the fact that there were still banks excluded from it. The alternative of using several fiscal agents could not solve the problem of discrimination among banks, and the closer the government approached this ideal—that is, the more fiscal agents it used—the greater were its ordinary expenses.

Nevertheless, Jackson in this passage was supporting the grievances of state banks against the Bank of the United States. Yet somewhat later in the message Jackson referred to the obligation imposed on the Second Bank by the recharter bill to redeem its notes at par when presented by state banks as "a bond of union among the banking establishments of the nation, erecting them into an interest separate from that of the people." In this passage, Jackson appeared to be opposed to all banks, not just the Bank of the United States, regarding their interests as opposed to those of other members of the economy. Consequently, it is not at all clear whether Jackson was opposed to the single Bank of the United States or to all banks. Both points of view found support among Jackson's advisers, and he apparently did not discriminate between them.

Leaving Jackson's objections to one side for the moment,

the currency-redemption provision itself was a bit curious. It obligated the Second Bank to redeem its notes at par at any branch, no matter where they were issued. When the bank was chartered in 1816, this policy was adopted. The notes often did not return to the issuing branches, and other branches found themselves unwittingly responsible for their redemption. The Western and Southern branches in particular were not called upon to redeem their notes, and there was no effective check on their issue. The abuse of this freedom was an important factor in the commercial crisis of 1819. And as a result of this embarrassment, the policy was suspended for several years.

To understand why the notes of Western and Southern branches migrated to the East, it is necessary to view the financial system of the time as a whole.[5] Trade—whether domestic or international—was carried on with the aid of extensive credit. It took a considerable amount of time to transport goods from where they were grown or made to where they would be consumed, and someone had to own these goods while they were in transit. If payment was made only when the goods were received, then the seller would have to bear the burden of carrying a large inventory, much of which would be in transit to purchasers at any moment of time. On the other hand, if payment was made at the time of shipment, then purchasers would have to pay for their goods well in advance of receiving them. Obviously, if some third party could be found to hold the goods or to extend credit to one of the parties, it would facilitate

5. The explanation usually given is inadequate. Govan, for example, says (p. 56), "The port cities of the Northeast were the principal markets within the nation, and the current of exchanges moved toward them from the South and the West. The notes issued by the interior branches, being acceptable everywhere in payment of debts to the United States, consequently found their way slowly but certainly to Philadelphia, New York, Boston, and Baltimore as they passed from hand to hand in regular settlement of individual transactions." All this is true, but it is only part of the story. The people of the South and West not only bought goods; they also sold them. The question that must be answered is why the sales of Southern and Western staples did not produce a contrary movement of Eastern notes to these regions or a return of their notes to them.

matters. This is exactly what happened, and a major part of the antebellum financial system was geared to provide credit for commercial transactions involving shipments of goods.

The shipment of goods raised another problem—the problem of exchange—and the antebellum financial system was geared to deal with this also. In addition to the time that elapsed between the sale of the goods and the time they were received by the buyer, there was also the distance they traveled. The buyer desired to pay at the place he received the goods, and the seller wished to be paid where he sold them. It was therefore necessary to transfer money from one place to the other.

Credit could be supplied either by itself or in the same financial instrument that provided exchange. To provide credit without exchange, a merchant obtained a loan or sold a commercial bill and then extended "book credit" to his customers. A commercial bill was simply a promise to pay a certain sum at some specified time in the future, typically 60 or 90 days. The person who bought the bill was paying money now for a promise to receive money in the future; in short, he was extending a loan. He was paid for this service by the difference between the price he paid for the bill and the amount of money he received when it came due. Since the amount to be paid when the bill came due was written on the bill, the purchaser subtracted the interest he charged from it to get the price he was willing to pay for the bill. The bill therefore was purchased at a discount, and the interest rate charged on it was referred to as the discount rate.

Pure exchange resulted from shipping money from place to place. Money consisted of the means of payment held by the public—coins (specie) and bank notes in the hands of the public and bank deposits owned by the public. Specie was valued everywhere, making it a desirable medium of exchange, but it was expensive to transport and in short supply. At the prevailing price level, there was not nearly enough specie to supply everyone's need for exchange. Bank notes and deposits were in more plentiful supply, but notes and checks drawn on bank deposits depreciated in value as they traveled from the issuing bank. For some banks and in some times, they depreciated less than the cost of shipping specie, and they were preferred to specie in these cases. International exchange, of course, could not be performed by shipping bank notes or checks, because American bank notes and deposits were not usable for purchases in Britain, and British notes could not be used in the United States.

Credit with exchange was supplied by means of a bill of exchange. This bill was a promise to pay at a future time and in a place different from the origin of the bill. It was used as follows· A seller of goods drew a bill of exchange on the buyer at the time of sale. This bill ordered the buyer to pay for the goods at a later time and at the place he would receive the goods. The buyer or his agent at the point of sale accepted the bill, signifying his agreement to pay it. It was then sold to a third party, typically a bank or merchant banking house. The purchaser was extending credit for the duration of the bill and transferring money from where the bill would be redeemed when it came due to where the bill was originally purchased. It charged for these services by paying less for the bill than the amount for which the bill was drawn, that is, by discounting it. The discount on a bill of exchange was the sum of the cost of exchange and the interest rate on the loan. Since there was no reason for the interest rate on bills of exchange to differ from the discount rate on commercial bills, the exchange rate between the place where the bill was bought and where it was drawn can be found by subtracting the discount rate from the discount on bills of exchange.

Exchange, of course, was a two-way operation, and it was not possible for the exchange to run completely in one direction. Consider the effects of a bill of exchange drawn for a shipment of cotton, drawn, let us say, in Charleston on New York or London. It was discounted by a bank in Charleston (the bank giving its notes in return), and remitted to New York or London, where it was sold or held until it came due. At the time it was sold or came due the Charleston bank acquired a credit in a New York or London bank (that is, it received either bank notes or, more typically, a deposit in a bank in those cities); although if the bill was drawn on London, it probably was sent to London via New York, the Charleston bank acquiring a credit in New York and a New York bank acquiring a credit in London. A Charleston bank could not continue indefinitely to pile up credits in New York; the funds would have to be spent. And the way they were spent was to finance purchases in New York of goods for people in Charleston; that is, they were used for exchange in the opposite direction.

These financial instruments were used variously. The shipment and export of Southern and Western staples was financed largely by bills of exchange.[6] The reverse shipment of Eastern manufactures and imports, however, was more often accomplished by book credit and shipment of Southern and Western bank notes to the East. To continue our example, when people in Charleston bought New York products, they paid with notes of a Charleston bank. These notes were shipped to New York, where they were deposited in banks, canceling the credits that the Charleston bank had accumulated through sale of bills of exchange. The eastward movement of bank notes that we set out to explain was the result.[7]

6. Bills were normally drawn for up to two thirds or three fourths of cotton shipments. Norman S. Buck, *The Development of the Organization of Anglo-American Trade, 1800–50* (New Haven: Yale University Press, 1925), pp. 12–13.

7. U. S. Congress, House Report 460, 22nd Congress, 1st Session (1832), pp. 316–17, 321. An alternate explanation, perhaps implicit in statements such as the one by Govan just cited, assumes that the abuse of the system about to be described was the norm. This view says that the South and West had a persistent balance-of-payments deficit with the East and that the flow of bank notes was the financial aspect of the capital flow from the East. There are no data with which to discriminate between these hypotheses, although the policy of the Second Bank (to be described shortly) of returning notes to the issuing bank for redemption in specie suggests that the accumulation of Southern and Western bank notes in the East was not a preferred method of financing

It is easy to see how this system was open to abuse. If the Charleston bank issued notes in return for local commercial bills or loans to local merchants, these notes could find their way to New York as easily as notes issued in return for a bill of exchange. If the notes were issued for a local loan, however, the issuing bank would not acquire a credit in New York. When the notes reached New York, banks in that city would find themselves with liabilities of the Charleston bank (that is, notes) without offsetting assets. They would have to ship the notes back to Charleston to obtain payment instead of simply subtracting their value from the Charleston bank's New York deposits. This was a laborious and uncertain process with the transportation and communication facilities of the time. The notes would not return to the Charleston bank till long after their issue, and there was no immediate check on its note issue. The excessive issue of the branches of the Second Bank in the South and West were able to lead the Bank into difficulty in 1819 because of this delay.

The possibility of abuse was well known, and there was no law obliging banks to take the notes of other banks. The notes were not legal tender, that is, specie, they were promises to pay legal tender upon presentation to the issuing bank. A bank note from a Charleston bank obviously was worth *no more* than its face value at New York. (It was only worth its face value in Charleston if the bank was redeeming its notes at par.) And if the Charleston bank did not have a credit with New York banks, anyone possessing the note in New York would have to transport it to Charleston to get specie for it. This entailed delay and transport cost, and there was the risk that the Charleston bank would refuse to pay for the note when it was presented. Notes of distant banks, like bills of exchange, were worth less than their face value, and they circulated at a discount.

---

a capital flow. Fishlow assumed explicitly that there were no interregional capital flows in his study of antebellum interregional trade. See Albert Fishlow, "Antebellum Interregional Trade Reconsidered," *American Economic Review, Papers and Proceedings,* LIV (May, 1964), 352–64.

On the other hand, if the Bank of the United States was required by law to redeem its notes at par at whatever branch they were presented to, its notes would not have this discount when they circulated far from the issuing branch. People would prefer to remit notes of the Bank of the United States in preference to notes of other banks because the notes would not diminish in value in transit. Bank of United States notes would thus be preferred to other bank notes for long-distance transactions, and they would act to confine other notes to a local circulation. This provision of the bill to recharter the Second Bank thus assured the other banks that the Second Bank would be a superior competitor in the issuing of notes. Far from being a bond of unity among banks, it would appear to create a bone of contention between them.

But why restrict the redemption privilege to banks? The new charter would have obligated the Second Bank to redeem its notes at par when presented by other banks, but not when presented by individuals. Yet if banks could redeem the notes at par at the local branch of the Bank of the United States, surely they would have paid the par value or very close to it for the notes. (Since the government received the notes at par in payment of duties and taxes, individuals would have paid the par value or close to it also.) The provision thus ensured that the notes would circulate at or near par; the restriction only put one additional minor step in the redemption process. This restriction may have been put in to reduce the force of the provision; at the same time as the Second Bank was forced to be a superior competitor, it was asked to work with its competition. If state banks were not able to issue their own notes easily, at least they could profit a little by purchasing Bank of United States notes at a slight discount and redeeming them at the Second Bank. This does not look like an important source of income, and it is hard to believe that the motivation of the restriction was to preserve it. Nevertheless, an amendment to broaden the redemption privilege was offered and rejected while the Senate was considering the recharter; the supporters of the Second Bank must have had some reason for the restriction.[8]

Returning to Jackson's statement, this provision was hardly a bond of unity among banks. It may have been supported by banks, however, as it simplified the process of transferring money within the country. The state banks were willing to give up some of their profits on issuing notes in return for greater regularity and predictability in domestic exchange.[9] This would not create an interest separate from that of the people; rather it would simplify the process of interregional trade. Nevertheless, Jackson's hostility to all banks in this connection conflicts with his sympathy for banks excluded from the Second Bank's monopoly of the domestic exchange.

Banks and the Sources of Capital

In addition to the question of the relation of the Second Bank to other banks, Jackson treated the question of sectionalism in his veto message. After commenting that little of the stock of the Second Bank was held in the West, Jackson said, "It is obvious that the debt of the people in that section [the West] to the bank [of the United States] is principally a debt to the Eastern and foreign stockholders; that the interest they pay upon it is carried into the Eastern States and into Europe, and that it is a burden upon their industry and a drain of their currency, which no country can bear without inconvenience and occasional distress."

There are two ways in which the Second Bank could have loaned money to people in the West. It could have purchased bills of that region, and it could have held Western bank notes. In the former case, the Second Bank would have issued its own currency in exchange for the purchased bill. In the latter, the

8. Catterall, p. 234.
9. Jean Alexander Wilburn, *Biddle's Bank: The Crucial Years* (New York: Columbia University Press, 1967), p. 46.

Second Bank would not have returned notes to the issuing bank, and this could be characterized as a drain of currency from the West. But it is clear that this drain would not have been a burden to the West; it would have been a means for the West to obtain loans from the East—in short, a benefit.

The balance sheet of the Second Bank in January, 1832, may give an index of the extent to which these two methods of extending credit were used. It is shown in Table 2.1. The Sec-

TABLE 2.1

Balance Sheet of the Bank of the United States,
January, 1832 (millions of dollars)

ASSETS		LIABILITIES	
Loans and discounts	66.3	Circulation (Notes)	21.4
Stock	—	Deposits	22.8
Real estate	2.1	Due to state banks	2.0
Banking houses	1.2	Capital	35.0
Due by state banks	3.9	Surplus *	1.5
Notes of state banks	2.2		82.7
Specie	7.0		
	82.7		

* Residual entered to make assets and liabilities equal; not in source.
SOURCE: *U. S. Congress, House Document 111, 26th Congress, 2nd Session (1841), p. 1418.*

ond Bank held 30 times as many loans and discounts (purchased bills) as notes of state banks. Most of the credit extended by the Second Bank was extended by purchasing bills; very little, by holding state bank notes. The Second Bank, therefore, did not drain currency from the West to any large degree, irrespective of whether this drain was a burden or a benefit.[10]

This, of course, was to be expected from the preceding discussion of the reasons why people in the West would have been

10. The volume of state bank notes held usually was even less than that shown in Table 2.1. U. S. Congress, Senate Document 128, 25th Congress, 2nd Session (1838), pp. 208–11.

more likely to remit notes of the Second Bank than other bank notes in making interregional transfers. It may be noted, however, that the balance sheet—which is a picture of the Bank's condition at an instant of time—does not give an index of the flow of state bank notes through the Bank. The Second Bank received many notes from state banks, but it quickly returned them to the issuing banks for payment, leaving only the small balance shown on hand at any moment. The Second Bank was not serving to drain currency from the West; it was returning the notes to the West as soon as they were received.

Returning to Jackson's point, it is curious to see him representing a drain of currency—whether or not it existed—as a burden. Any drain would represent loans to the region losing currency. This region could then issue more bank notes, let them drain away, and thereby secure more loans. Unless we are prepared to dismiss Jackson's statement as nonsense, the only reasonable interpretation to give it is that he viewed loans as a burden. Loans, of course, can be a burden, but only if the borrowing was unwise. Jackson may have been saying that the inhabitants of the West needed to be protected from themselves, that they should be denied the facilities through which to borrow money in order that they should not borrow unwisely. Those who wished to borrow unwisely would be precluded from doing so, but those who wished to borrow with reason—to finance interregional or international trade or to finance the growth of industry or agriculture—would be denied the opportunity also. The West would be protected from unwise borrowing at a Draconian cost.

Whether or not this was Jackson's aim, refusing a new charter to the Second Bank would not have achieved it. The Second Bank was the principal dealer in domestic exchange, but if the Second Bank had not existed, other means would have been found to transfer credit from one place to another. The government, in fact, would have had to ensure that this was possible to carry out its normal functions, dooming any policy of regional self-sufficiency to failure. If the Second Bank had not existed, people dealing in domestic exchange would have had to deal with many banks, not just one, increasing—not decreasing—the opportunity for unwise borrowing.

Jackson does not merely talk of interregional debt in the statement quoted; he talks of debt to the stockholders of the Second Bank. It is not accurate, however, to talk of bank debt as debts to the owners of the banks, and we must examine the balance sheet of the Second Bank (Table 2.1) more closely to see why.

The investors who owned the Second Bank provided only $35 million for its operations, even if the capital shown in the balance sheet was fully paid up. As the loans and discounts were almost double this amount, the Second Bank's stockholders could not have extended all of them. In fact, the Bank's loans and discounts exceeded the contribution of the stockholders by more than has been suggested by this brief statement, for not all of the shares of the Bank's stock were purchased with specie. The charter required only that one quarter of the stock be purchased with specie, and many of the shares were purchased with loans, particularly from the Second Bank itself. Since the purchase of stock with a loan from the Second Bank did not represent an increase in the Bank's liquid assets, the contribution of the stockholders was far less than the capital shown, and the loans that cannot be traced back to specie contributions by the stockholders far exceeded the surplus of loans and discounts over capital.[11]

When a bank extended loans, either by negotiating individual loans or by discounting commercial bills and bills of exchange, there were two possibilities. The bank could extend these loans by paying its specie to the borrowers. In this case, the value added to the assets of the bank by the loans and discounts would be exactly offset by a fall in the specie hold-

11. William M. Gouge, *An Inquiry into the Principles of the American Banking System* (Philadelphia, 1833), pp. 70–73; Catterall, p. 29. The Second Bank never had more than $3 million in specie during its first two years of operation. This is even less than its charter required.

ings, preserving—as it must be preserved in this type of accounting—the equality of assets and liabilities plus net worth. This would be a loan by the stockholders to the bank's customers. The bank, in fact, would then be nothing more than an intermediary between lenders and borrowers, an important function of a bank, but not the only one. By the use of "fractional reserves," a bank could extend its operations beyond the role of a broker; this was the second possible means of treating loans and discounts.

Instead of giving borrowers gold and silver for their loans, the bank could have given them notes or opened deposits for them. The distinguishing feature of a banking corporation was its ability to issue bank notes, and the contemporary discussion of banks centered on this activity. But banks could also give deposits to its customers, in the same way as commercial banks have deposits today. A depositor would then pay his debt by check instead of by bank note, and the effect would be the same: the check, like notes, would be presented to the issuing bank for specie or the settlement of inter-bank balances. It has been thought that deposits were not widely used at this time, but the data for the Second Bank in Table 2.1 shows this not to be the case. Notes were used very extensively in the South and West, deposits were more important in urban areas. For the country as a whole, the value of deposits was only slightly less than the value of bank notes during the 1830's, and the reverse had long been true in the major cities of the country.[12]

If the bank followed this second option, the loans and discounts would represent a net addition to the assets, offset by an addition of either notes—that is, circulation—or deposits to the liabilities. Notes and deposits were liabilities because they were *promises to pay* specie on demand. Under the first alternative (paying out specie), the loans and discounts could not exceed the original accumulation of specie, which was no larger than

12. J. Van Fenstermaker, *The Development of American Commercial Banking, 1782–1837* (Kent, Ohio: Kent State University, 1965), pp. 41, 67; Hammond, pp. 80–83.

the capital. Under the second alternative, such a constraint did not exist, and the loans and discounts could exceed the value of the capital—as shown in Table 2.1. There was, in fact, no formal limit to the value of loans and discounts or the concomitant sum of circulation and deposits. Each bank could loan as much as it wanted—that is, issue as many notes or deposits as it wanted —subject only to the qualification that it remain solvent. The Second Bank, for example, could not legally issue more notes than its capital, but there was no restriction on its deposits.

The threat to solvency from overissue of notes or deposits originated in the character of these instruments. They were current liabilities of the bank, representing promises by the bank to pay specie on demand. If the circulation and deposits of a bank totaled more than its specie, then if all the holders of these notes and deposits converged on the bank at once and demanded payment, the bank would be unable to comply. It would have to refuse to honor its obligations. Clearly, if a bank had less specie than the total value of its notes and deposits, it was acting on the assumption that not all of these liabilities would be presented for payment at one time. Each bank made an assumption—explicitly or implicitly—about the frequency with which its notes and deposits would return for redemption and held reserves appropriately. (As notes could be expected to circulate more widely than checks before being returned to the bank, banks could hold fewer reserves for notes than for deposits.[13]) But reserves represented idle cash, and there was a great incentive not to hold too many—money could be used to earn more money. Stated another way, there was an incentive to underestimate the amount of specie reserves needed for every dollar of circulation or deposit and to decrease the ratio of reserves to notes and deposits below the limits of prudence.

13. Early checks apparently were used both for the functions of modern checks and as bills of exchange. See Fritz Redlich and Webster M. Christman, "Early Checks and an Example of Their Use," *Business History Review*, XLI (Autumn, 1967), 285–302, and James P. Baughman, "Early American Checks: Forms and Functions," *Business History Review*, XLI (Winter, 1967), 421–35, especially 431.

Nevertheless, the bank had given to the recipient of the loan a means of payment that he had not had before, and he would purchase something with it. (He presumably obtained the loan for this purpose.) Anyone who sold things to him would receive bank notes or a check in return for his wares, and he could redeem them for specie, hold them (that is, hold the notes or deposit the check in a bank), or spend them. In the first case, the bank would have lost specie just as if it had given specie to the recipient of the loan directly. As we noted, this would be a loan by the stockholders, but there were far too many loans for all the outstanding notes and checks to have been redeemed in specie. In the second case, the seller would have exchanged his goods for a bank obligation—that is, he would have foregone command over his goods temporarily. He would have extended credit to the bank by increasing his holdings of bank obligations —notes and deposits—and he would have been the source of the bank's loan. In the third case, there would be a new seller holding the notes or checks, and he would have the same options as the first one.

If, at the end of this chain, the new notes and deposits had all been redeemed for specie, there would have been no increase in the money supply, and the stockholders would have extended the loan. On the other hand, if some people were willing to hold more bank obligations than before, they would have accepted a claim on resources for these resources themselves. They would have allowed others to use their resources in return for a promise to give them the resources or their equivalent back at some future time; they would have extended the loan. We do not know who these individuals were, but there is no reason to think that they were stockholders of the bank making loans.

We therefore cannot identify those people who extended loans to people in the West and South, although it is true that the Second Bank received payment for its services in handling such of these transactions as it did. As in the case of the relation of the Second Bank to state banks, Jackson commented on an aspect of the banking structure without comprehending its significance. In the former case, we could not tell if Jackson was protecting the people from all banks or from the Bank of the United States. Here we cannot tell if Jackson was protecting the people of the West from the inhabitants of the East or from themselves. His rhetoric supports the former; the logic of his argument, the latter.

The Second Bank as a Central Bank

These are the major economic arguments of the veto message. The arguments about the constitutionality of the Second Bank and its supposed control by foreigners (or, alternatively, by a small group of natives as a result of the nonvoting status of foreign stockholders) add little to our understanding of the economic issues in Jackson's opposition. He said in his summary: "We can at least take a stand against all new grants of monopolies and exclusive privileges, against any prostitution of our Government to the advancement of the few at the expense of the many," but the connection between these sentiments and the operation of the Second Bank is open to question. Without attempting to judge the issue of Jackson's ultimate motivation, this economic analysis of his veto message certainly supports the conclusion of Marvin Meyers: "The Bank was called a Monster by Jacksonians. A monster is an unnatural thing, its acts are out of reason, and its threats cannot be estimated in ordinary practical terms. The effort to destroy the Monster Bank and its vicious brood—privileged corporations, paper money—enlisted moral passions in a drama of social justice and self-justification." [14]

14. Meyers, pp. 10–11. The lack of economic coherence in the message informs us about Jackson's advisers as well as about the President himself. "Kendall's authorship of the veto message suggests that its ambiguities in formal ideological statement are beside the point. Kendall did not try to set forth logically consistent doctrine *per se;* rather he probed for the popular mind, as he had learned in Kentucky in the 1820's." Lynn L. Marshall, "The Authorship of Jackson's Bank Veto Message," *Journal of American History,* L (December, 1963), 477.

Nevertheless, this effort obviously had economic consequences, and it is appropriate to evaluate it as an economic measure. Later chapters will deal with its immediate impact. Here we pose a question of a more long-run nature: Was the Second Bank of the United States a central bank? [15]

There does not seem to be a generally accepted definition of a central bank, but there does seem to be general agreement that a central bank should perform two roles. In normal times, the central bank should act to facilitate commerce and to regulate the markets for money and credit. In times of crisis, the central bank should act to restore confidence by being a "lender of last resort." We consider these in turn.

The first of these functions is somewhat amorphous. There are many things that can be done to make the economy move easily, and it is not clear how many of them a bank needs to perform to become a true central bank. The Second Bank under Biddle did a variety of things that fit this classification. It arranged for payments of the government debt in ways that insulated commerce from these shocks. It arranged for interregional transfers of government funds without strain on state banks. It tried, on occasion, to neutralize the effects of rapid international specie flows. [16]

Two functions of the Bank may be isolated as having primary importance in this regard. The Second Bank of the United States was chartered at a time when the state banks had suspended specie payments—that is, when they had refused to redeem their notes in specie at par. The government, which had to transfer money from state to state, could not fulfill its obliga-

15. This question has been posed by many authors, particularly Esther Rogoff Taus, *Central Banking Functions of the United States Treasury, 1789–1941* (New York: Columbia University Press, 1943); Fritz Redlich, *The Molding of American Banking: Men and Ideas* (New York: Hafner Publishing Co., 1951); Smith; and Hammond. The question evaluates the Second Bank by modern, as opposed to contemporary, standards. Obviously, other standards could be used. See below, pp. 57–58.

16. Redlich, pp. 125–35; Smith, pp. 134–46.

tions, and the Second Bank was chartered to retrieve the government by inducing state banks to resume specie payments. In addition to restoring the redemption of notes at par at their place of issue, the new Bank of the United States also tried to ensure the circulation of notes at par at locations other than the point of issue. As stated above, the Bank moved in this direction by offering to redeem the notes of any of its branches at any other branch.

These efforts, however, were not initially successful. More exactly, they were initially successful, but the establishment of the Second Bank was followed by a crash in which the Bank figured prominently. We have already noted that the normal flow of bank notes was from West and South to the East, and when the Second Bank announced that all notes would be redeemed at all branches, notes from the Southern and Western branches of the Bank were presented for redemption at the Eastern branches. There was no check on the issue of the Western and Southern branches; their notes returned to other branches, not to them. The managers of these branches did not respond to appeals to restrict their discounts, and the management of the branch at Baltimore took advantage of the general confusion to emulate them. As a result, the liabilities of the Second Bank grew without control.

In the summer of 1818, two years after the establishment of the Second Bank, the directors realized that the Bank was overextended. They rescinded the order making notes of the Bank redeemable at all branches, and they began to curtail the Bank's operations. Within a few months there was a banking panic, leading to severe deflation and depression. Catterall commented the the Second Bank's "Curtailments had, indeed, precipitated the panic, for which, however, it was hardly more responsible than was Noah for the flood." [17] The aptness of Catterall's simile may be questioned, but his general reasoning is sound. There was a rapid deflation in England, and there was bound to be some reaction to the shifting of demands after the War of

17. Catterall, p. 61.

1812. Nevertheless, the severity of the crisis may not have been inevitable. If there had been no Bank of the United States, or if there had been a better-managed Bank of the United States, the crisis might have been less of a crisis and more of a gradual deflation. The parallel to the deflation after 1839 is striking. In each case, prices in the United States had to fall to bring them into line with prices in England; and in each case, the Bank of the United States was blamed.

But even if the role of the Second Bank is agreed upon, there is still an additional question to be answered. For if the Second Bank could not have avoided expansion in 1817 and 1818—due to institutional constraints or political pressure—then the management of the Bank cannot be held responsible for its role in the panic, even if that role was major. The Secretary of the Treasury in particular must bear a portion of the blame for the Panic of 1819. He persuaded the Bank of the United States to make a bad compact with the state banks in order to induce them to resume specie payments. The Second Bank agreed to act as if it had received government funds on deposit with the state banks, but not to actually receive them for five months. It agreed not to collect balances owed to it by the state banks until it had considerably expanded its business. And it agreed to accept checks on other state banks in payment for these debts. In other words, the Second Bank agreed to conduct its business as if it could collect the debts owed to it without actually collecting them. It could not obtain the government deposits it had to service, and it could collect private debts only by incurring other debts, at first because it had to expand its discounts and then because it was obligated to accept checks of one bank in payment of debts of another.

In addition, the Second Bank was hampered in those efforts it did make to curtail the activities of state banks. The Treasury resisted any pressure on state banks in an effort to maintain specie payments, and state courts and legislatures did likewise in an effort to protect local businessmen. Although the management of the Second Bank was not blameless, the Treasury's

pressure on the Bank was as important as the independent actions of the Bank in the expansion leading to the crisis. The
cause of the Panic of 1819 was the banking structure that allowed each state to strike out on its own and the financial
necessities of the Federal Government that placed it at the
mercy of state banks.[18]

This glimpse of the early history of the Second Bank of the
United States is important for several reasons. Whatever the
correct view of the period, contemporaries were convinced that
the Second Bank was culpable. This is typified in Gouge's often
quoted statement about the attempts of the Bank to curtail its
activities in 1818: "The Bank was saved and the people were
ruined." [19] This hostility never disappeared, even though the
Second Bank's management in 1832 bore no relation to the
management in 1818. In addition, this episode raises the question of the relationship between the Bank of the United States
and the Treasury. It is not clear whether the Bank had the
power to work independently of the Treasury, or whether it was
simply a means through which the Treasury exerted its influence. To the extent that it was the latter, its role as fiscal agent
of the government was more important than its central banking
activities.[20]

In any case, the Second Bank began the long process of
rebuilding itself and public confidence. The policy of redeeming
the Bank's notes at any branch was abandoned and replaced by
the defensive policy of paying out notes of other banks whenever possible. This policy defended the Bank because the Bank
constantly received new supplies of notes of other banks from
the government, which had received them in payment of duties
or taxes. If the Bank paid with them instead of its own notes, it

18. Leon M. Schur, "The Second Bank of the United States and the
Inflation after the War of 1812," *Journal of Political Economy,* LXVIII
(April, 1960), 118–134; Catterall, pp. 24–26; Hammond, pp. 249–50.

19. Quoted, for example, in Catterall, p. 61, and Hammond, p. 259.

20. See Richard H. Timberlake, Jr., "The Specie Standard and
Central Banking in the United States before 1860," *Journal of Economic
History,* XXI (September, 1961), 318–41.

did not expand its own liabilities, and it ran little risk of depleting its specie reserves.

The cost of this defense was severe. As the Second Bank was paying out notes of state banks in return for bills discounted, it could not return these notes to the issuing bank for redemption. The Second Bank therefore had no means of control over the state banks.

Nicholas Biddle, when he assumed the presidency of the Second Bank in 1823, set out to restore the original policy of issuing the Bank's own notes. In order for the Second Bank to issue its own notes, it had to return state bank notes to the issuing bank for redemption. If it did not do so, it would accumulate balances of state bank notes—an asset of doubtful liquidity—to offset its highly liquid liability of bank notes. If it did, state banks would be prevented from issuing more notes than they could redeem, and the Second Bank would have established some measure of control over them. As a result of this control, discounts on state bank notes would fall as the expectation of easy redemption increased. People would then use these notes for interregional transfers instead of using only the Second Bank's notes, and the Second Bank could resume its offer to redeem its notes at any branch without fear of inundation in the East.[21]

The effects of this policy appear mostly in the rates of discounts for Western bank notes. Using discounts on notes at Philadelphia—the home of the Second Bank—as a guide, we find the following experience. The discounts on New England notes fell continuously, but not very far. With the exception of notes from Maine, New England notes never sold at a discount of more than 5 percent. This narrowed to about 1 percent in the late 1820's, but for reasons that have little to do with the Second Bank. The Second Bank did not do very much business in New England, and the banking system in that region was highly sophisticated. The increasing quality of New England

21. Catterall, pp. 96–98. Biddle's predecessor, Cheves, had also redeemed state bank notes for specie on a regular basis. *Ibid.,* p. 77.

notes was the result of the policies of the Suffolk Bank (to be described shortly), not of the Bank of the United States.

Discounts on relatively poor notes from Middle Atlantic and Southeastern states fell from something over 5 percent in the early 1820's to something under 5 percent a decade later; high-quality notes from these regions sold near par throughout the period. Discounts on notes from Western and Southwestern banks stayed around 5 percent, but notes from Tennessee, Kentucky, and Alabama went from being sold at great discounts—25 percent or more—to being accepted at the rates applicable to neighboring states. Although notes of distant banks did not circulate at par in Philadelphia, there was beginning to be a "national currency" usable without too much difficulty.[22]

We therefore must discriminate between the periods before and after Biddle's accession to the presidency of the Second Bank. During the first period—despite initial attempts to do more—the Second Bank of the United States was merely a large bank. It acted as the government's fiscal agent, but its management was too frightened to take any responsibility for the state of the currency or the economy. Nicholas Biddle acknowledged this responsibility when he became head of the Second Bank in 1823, and the Second Bank acted thereafter to produce a national currency by the symbiotic policies of issuing its own notes and rapidly redeeming the notes of other banks that it received.

There are three points to be noted about this policy. First, it was a deflationary policy. It restricted the volume of notes a bank could issue without depleting its reserves, but that is all it

22. Jonathan Elliot, *The Funding System of the United States and Great Britain* (Washington, 1845), pp. 1106–28 (printed also as U. S. Congress, House Document 15, 28th Congress, 1st Session; Sumner, p. 198; Catterall, pp. 442–44; Van Fenstermaker, pp. 77–95. A list of discounts, however, does not give a true measure of the currency. There were difficulties in dealing with myriad bank notes of varying quality, and the simple problem of obtaining information was formidable. A *Bank Note Reporter and Counterfeit Detector* of 1830 listed the current discount in New York on notes of 500 banks and the names of perhaps twice that number of counterfeit, altered, and spuriously signed notes. William H. Dillistin, *Bank Note Reporters and Counterfeit Detectors, 1826–1866* (New York: American Numismatic Society, 1949), p. 99.

did. It was a substitute for a legal reserve requirement, even though the restrictions on bank activities were not as strict as a legal requirement would have been.[23]

Second, this policy was not unique to the Second Bank. The Suffolk Bank of Boston also redeemed notes as soon as it received them unless banks had agreed to maintain a balance at the Suffolk Bank for that purpose. The Suffolk Bank thus did for New England what the Bank of the United States was attempting to do for the rest of the country. The Suffolk Bank was a private bank, which shows that the policy in question was not dependent on government support. The bank redeeming or threatening to redeem notes needed only to have a source of notes to use. The Bank of the United States was the fiscal agent of the government, and it received from the government the notes paid to the government by individuals. The Suffolk Bank was a clearing house for several large Boston banks, and it acquired the notes paid to those banks.[24]

These two banks were specially situated, but all banks received notes of other banks and could present them for redemption. Why could not any bank regulate its fellows? Clearly, only a large bank could be an effective regulator. And more important than mere size was the volume of notes flowing into the bank. The Bank of the United States was particularly well suited to be an effective constraint on other banks—both because of its large size and its position as fiscal agent of the government—but it was by no means the only bank that could adopt the policy.

A problem must be raised at this point. What was to prevent

23. Hammond, p. 277, asserted that a central bank in an expanding economy had to be mostly "negative," that is, deflationary. This assertion seems to be based on Hammond's moralistic view of enterprise (see his comment, p. 275), a view that led him to claim, p. 573, that prices *rose* "persistently though haltingly" under the National Banking Act.

24. See the discussion of the Suffolk Bank in Redlich, I, 67–87, especially 71, where Redlich recognized that the power of the Suffolk Bank derived from its threat to present notes for redemption, even though various institutional forms obviated the use of this power in most cases.

banks, when presented with their notes for redemption by the
Second Bank, from presenting to the Second Bank its notes in
return? Clearly, nothing. Notes of the Second Bank could be
counted as reserves by individual banks fearing the Second
Bank's policy of presenting notes for redemption. Therefore, if
the Second Bank wanted to affect the ratio of monetary liabilities to *specie* reserves, it had to ensure that the state banks did
not have as many of its obligations as it had of theirs. Monetary
obligations, of course, included deposits as well as notes, and a
bank could cancel a debt to the Second Bank as easily as return
its notes. Consequently, the Bank of the United States had to
issue its notes and deposits less freely than an ordinary bank
would have done—that is, it had to maintain a reserve of bank
debts owed to it against its liabilities as well as a reserve of
specie. As the balance sheet in Table 2.1 shows, the Second
Bank had such a dual reserve in 1832. It owed state banks $2.0
million, but the state banks owed to the Second Bank $6.1
million—the sum of their balances with the Second Bank and
the value of their notes held by the Second Bank.[25]

The third point to be noted about the policy of rapid note
redemption is that it was not discretionary. The Second Bank
could police the state banks, but if it did so, it gave up the
discretionary power to either increase or decrease the volume of
money by varying the rate of note redemption. If the Second
Bank allowed the supply of money to expand by accumulating a
balance of state bank notes, it thereby relaxed its policing function. And since the Second Bank was returning notes to the
issuing bank for redemption as fast as possible in ordinary
times, there was no way for it to induce more contraction in
other banks by this means.[26] If the Bank of the United States
wished to preserve its policing function, therefore, it could affect
the supply of money only in the same ways open to other banks.

25. This was a typical condition. U. S. Congress, Senate Document
128, 25th Congress, 2nd Session (1838), pp. 208–11.
26. There were daily settlements in the major cities. Govan, pp.
85–86.

Because it was a large bank, it would have a large impact on the supply of money, but this impact would not differ from the impact of any other large bank. And only if the Bank of the United States was willing to lose its creditor status vis-à-vis other banks and consequently its opportunity to police them, could it expand the currency.[27]

In fact, the Bank of the United States in normal times assumed the role of policing the state banks rather than controlling the volume of money. In terms of modern institutions, it assumed a role performed by the Comptroller of the Currency in the late 19th century and now jointly by the Comptroller, the Federal Reserve, and the Federal Deposit Insurance Corporation.[28] As such, it was an important administrative agency of the government, but not a central bank.

Now let us turn to the question of the Second Bank's actions in crises. A central bank is supposed to act in crises as well as in normal times—a central bank's role in crisis being probably its most important defining characteristic. The essence of a crisis was the withdrawal of trust in the banking system by the public, and they all followed the same pattern. People became unwilling to hold bank obligations, fearing that banks would default on them. They attempted to exchange their bank notes or deposits for specie, exerting pressure on the banks, which did not have specie reserves equal to their liabilities. In order to get more specie—or some asset that would have replaced specie in the minds of the public—the banks called in their loans, hoping they would be paid at least partially in coin. Their debtors found it hard to pay off these loans in a time of stress, and the strain on them intensified the general lack of confidence in the

27. Biddle's attempts to introduce a small amount of discretion into this function must be placed in this context. His minor indulgence of state banks in April, 1825—cited by Hammond, p. 308—must be contrasted with his severity in October of that year, to be described below.

28. Lester V. Chandler, *The Economics of Money and Banking,* 4th ed. (New York: Harper and Row, 1964), pp. 144, 179–80. The Comptroller still regulates all national banks in accordance with informal agreements between it and the other regulators. *Ibid.,* p. 591.

monetary structure. More people demanded specie for bank
notes or deposits, and the crisis deepened.

A central bank would have short-circuited this procedure by
lending to the beleaguered banks. It would have supplied specie
to the banks if it had specie, or—if it did not have specie—its
notes might have done as well. In either case, the banks would
not have had to call in loans to get the means to redeem their
notes or deposits, and they would not have encouraged the
general distrust. When people saw that the banks could pay off
their obligations, they would once again have been willing to
hold these obligations, and the crisis would have subsided. Because a central bank lends to banks when the banks cannot
borrow elsewhere, it is called a "lender of last resort."

In the time between Biddle's accession to the presidency of
the Second Bank in 1823 and Jackson's veto of the recharter
bill in 1832, there was only one crisis serious enough to need a
lender of last resort. This was the crisis of 1825, and the actions
of the Bank in this crisis have been cited by investigators trying
to show it was a central bank.

The literature does not assign a cause to the small expansion that led to the crisis of 1825, but it was part of a world-
wide movement in 1824–25. The Secretary of the Treasury
moved to relieve the stringency existing in the money market in
late 1824 by early repayment of government debt falling due
January 1, 1825. This action did relieve the market, but as the
expansion resulted in a panic the following year, the wisdom of
this action may be questioned. Nevertheless, there can be no
doubt that the Treasury was performing a central banking function.[29]

According to Redlich, a modern supporter of the Second
Bank, Biddle realized the severity of the situation in April,
1825, and started to prepare for a crisis. The Second Bank sold
government securities and in other ways increased its reserves.
When the expected crisis came in July, 1825, Biddle was in a

29. Taus, pp. 30–31; Margaret G. Myers, *The New York Money
Market* (New York: Columbia University Press, 1931), I, 160–61.

position to help the banking community. Redlich stated: "There can be no doubt that for some critical weeks in 1825 Biddle acted as the lender of last resort, thereby fulfilling a true central banking function." But Redlich added that the Bank was careful not to fall into debt to the state banks and that it was willing to sell government securities.[30]

These qualifications are very important. Biddle apparently was not willing to forego even temporarily the Second Bank's role as regulator of state banks in favor of the central banking function. The lender of last resort thus had to restrict its loans so as not to become a net debtor. The willingness to sell government securities also worked against the Bank's main policy. In a crisis, the central bank should act to bring money into circulation, enabling debts to be settled without a cumulative banking contraction. Selling government securities withdrew money from circulation and acted to encourage the crisis. Redlich defended the Second Bank's policy on the grounds that government securities were bought from hoards—as opposed to funds active in commerce—and that banks were not sensitive to their reserve position in any case.[31] This defense is not convincing. First, it is hard to believe that *all* purchases of government securities were made from hoards, and the actions of the Secretary of the Treasury in prepaying part of the public debt assumed just the opposite; namely, that at least some of the money acquired would be spent and not hoarded. Second, although banks did not use reserve ratios as modern banks do, nevertheless they were sensitive to their reserve position. To use another inference, it is only in this case that the Second Bank's pressure against bank reserves through its presentation of notes for redemption has any meaning.

The other principal defender of the Second Bank as a central bank, Bray Hammond, recounted that the Bank was the agent in the government's repayment of seven million dollars of the public debt in October, 1825. Since the Second Bank made

30. Redlich, I, 135–36.
31. *Ibid.,* p. 137.

this payment by extending its own obligations—that is, since it paid with its own notes and checks—it became indebted to the state banks. To correct this situation the Bank sold its holdings of government bonds, carrying on the policy for four weeks until it was secure.[32] The Second Bank was engaging in deflationary actions at exactly the time when inflationary movements were needed. It was withdrawing money from circulation to strengthen its reserves at a time when it should have been putting money into circulation to ease the crisis. Even if some of the Bank's new reserves came from hoards, the effect of its sales was still deflationary.

The result of all this was that "a sharp drop occurred in the total of Bank credit outstanding in November, 1825, just when the business community would have been most grateful for an expansive policy." We may paraphrase the comment with which W. B. Smith followed this observation by saying that Biddle *and his supporters* have erred in exaggerating the helpfulness of the Second Bank in this emergency.[33]

The Bank of the United States, therefore, gets a higher rating on its aspirations to be a central bank than on its accomplishments. It helped to regulate the banking sector, but it was hampered by this regulatory function in its attempts to alleviate crises. It was unwilling to abandon temporarily its control over state banks in order to support them in the crisis of 1825, and it consequently never functioned as a lender of last resort. Nevertheless, the Second Bank was probably as close to being a central bank as any bank of its day, and this judgment should not be interpreted to mean that there was no room for improve-

32. Hammond, p. 310. See also Catterall, p. 107, and Smith, p. 139. Smith, like Redlich, said only that the Second Bank was in danger of falling into debt to the state banks. Biddle's account of the sales can be found in U. S. Congress, House Report 460, 22nd Congress, 1st Session (1832), pp. 434–35. He said the Second Bank was actually in debt to the state banks.

33. Smith, p. 140. The Treasury's repayment of the public debt, of course, did serve to alleviate the crisis, to the extent that it was not offset by the Second Bank's actions.

ment. The veto of the Bank foreclosed this possibility, and it is lamented on these grounds by the supporters of the Bank.[34]

But even if the Second Bank had been a true central bank, would that have been desirable? It seems heretical to challenge this underlying assumption in most discussions, but there are a few points to be raised. It is assumed that a central bank would have acted to eliminate or at least reduce the severity of business fluctuations, but a recent study of the actions of the Federal Reserve in 1929–33 casts some doubt on the reliability of this prediction.[35] In addition, it is taken for granted that business fluctuations were bad. We will present evidence in Chapter 5 suggesting that the depression of the early 1840's was not nearly as bad as has been thought. If the depression did not produce massive unemployment and loss of income, then it is quite possible that the costs of preventing it could have been greater than the costs of the depression. In particular, if the only way to avoid crises was to reduce sharply the rate of economic growth, the economy was probably better off with crises than without them.

This is not to suggest that all central banks are bad and that all economics in all times would be better off without them. It is, instead, a mild caveat to the use of modern standards to evaluate historical events. Central banks are modern institutions, and they operate today in a context very different from that of the nineteenth century. We like to think that the knowledge we have accumulated and the theories that we have formulated would have been of some use to our predecessors, but it does not necessarily follow that modern institutions controlled by men unfamiliar with modern ideas would have been of value. In fact, it is hard to see how any bank managed by men of the early nineteenth century could have fulfilled the role of a mod-

34. Smith, p. 254; Hammond, p. 346.
35. Milton Friedman and Anna Jacobson Schwartz, *A Monetary History of the United States, 1867–1960* (Princeton: Princeton University Press, 1963). Chapter 7 published separately as *The Great Contraction.*

ern central bank, for the simple reason that this role is the product of late nineteenth and twentieth century ideas. Nicholas Biddle sometimes talked like a modern central banker, but it would have been a superhuman effort for him to have taken the Second Bank far enough out of its contemporary setting to make it into a true central bank.[36]

36. It is worth noting that the Second Bank's founders and supporters generally did not support it on central banking grounds. See Timberlake, 1961, on this point, and Frank Whitson Fetter, *Development of British Monetary Orthodoxy, 1797–1875* (Cambridge: Harvard University Press, 1965), for an analysis of the Bank of England at this time.

3

Contraction and Inflation

~~~~~~

THE BANK of the United States had restrained the state banks; when this restraint was removed, according to the traditional account, unbridled expansion was the result. The state banks had been chafing at the bit before 1832, according to this story, and the "destruction" of the Second Bank allowed them to run wild. It was assumed—then as now—that the state banks *needed* an external restraint to preserve sensible banking standards.[1] But this assumption is not true; it overstates the effects of the Second Bank and it misrepresents the nature of the inflation after 1832. To discover what actually happened, we must examine the events of the 1830's in some detail.

"Biddle's Contraction"

Having refused a new charter to the Second Bank of the United States, Jackson began his second Administration with a plan to remove the government's deposits from the Bank. He

1. Roger B. Taney, then Secretary of the Treasury, stated this thesis in order to deny its validity in an 1834 report: "One of the arguments most frequently urged in favor of the expediency of a Bank of the United States, is the salutory influence which it is supposed to exert in securing to the country a sound currency. It is said that the State banks have a constant tendency to overissues, and that a superior power is necessary to keep them in check, and to control them in this particular; and the argument is constantly and earnestly pressed, that a Bank of the United States is the fit and appropriate means to accomplish this object." *Report on Deposit Banks,* 1834, in U. S. Treasury, *Reports by the Secretary,* III, 451.

would by this means achieve two aims. First, he would deprive the Second Bank of a substantial part of its business, since the government's deposits amounted to about one third of the Bank's monetary liabilities (deposits and circulation), and the government's business loomed large in the Bank's exchange dealings.[2] Second, he would deprive the Second Bank of its main source of state bank notes. It will be recalled from the last chapter that the Second Bank's ability to be an effective policeman of state banks depended on its ability to acquire large volumes of state bank notes. If the Bank was not the government's fiscal agent, it would also be a less effective policeman.

The Second Bank could still have pursued its policing function, albeit with diminished effect, if it chose. But in March, 1834, Biddle wrote to a colleague that "the Executive, by removing the public revenues, has relieved the Bank from all responsibility for the currency." [3] Biddle was talking about a political concept—responsibility—not his ability to pursue certain policies. From a purely economic point of view, the Second Bank could have followed the example of the Suffolk Bank by pursuing a policy of control as a private organization. From a political view, such a policy was unthinkable, and Biddle did not attempt it.

Jackson had appointed a new Secretary of the Treasury, William Duane, in June, 1833, specifically for the purpose of removing the deposits. But when Jackson asked Duane to remove the deposits, he refused, trying instead to convince Jackson of the folly of his course. The result was the dismissal of Duane and the appointment in his place of Roger B. Taney, a firm supporter of the President's policy, at the end of September, 1833.

The public deposits in the Bank of the United States had stayed near $10 million from 1828 to the start of 1833. They then fell to a low of $6.5 million in July, before returning to

2. Catterall, p. 503.
3. Nicholas Biddle, *Correspondence*. R. C. McGrane, ed. (Boston: Houghton Mifflin, 1919), pp. 225–26.

$10 million again in October. This fluctuation appears to have nothing to do with the government's removal of the deposits. The order for the removal was issued at the end of September to take effect October 1, and the public deposits in the Bank of the United States fell by almost $6 million in the last three months of 1833. The Second Bank thus lost *three fifths* of the government's deposits in three months; the remainder was withdrawn at a slower rate.[4]

The Second Bank responded to the Administration's actions by curtailing credit. There was discussion at the time, and there has been discussion since, on whether the Bank was justified in this policy. If deposits are withdrawn, any bank must curtail its operations. But to leap from here to the assertion that the magnitude and duration of Biddle's contraction was warranted is a difficult matter. It is made even more difficult by Biddle's avowed aim of forcing recharter of the Bank through economic hardship.[5] Without judging Biddle's actions, let us note a few of the provocations for it.

One point of friction between the Bank of the United States and the Administration antedated the removal of the deposits. A treaty had been negotiated in 1831 and ratified in February, 1832, in which France agreed to pay the United States an indemnity for "unlawful seizures, captures, sequestrations, confiscations, or destruction of . . . [American] cargoes, or other property," during the recent wars. The payment was supposed to be paid in six annual installments, beginning one year after ratification.[6] Accordingly, the United States Treasury drew a bill on the French Treasury in February, 1833, and sold it to the Second Bank. When presented with the bill, the French refused

4. Martin Van Buren, "Autobiography," *Annual Report of the American Historical Association for 1918* (Washington: Government Printing Office, 1920), p. 725; Remini, pp. 124–25; U. S. Congress, Senate Document 128, 25th Congress, 2nd Session (1838), p. 209. The public deposits were the sum of those credited to the United States Treasurer and those credited to Public Officers.

5. Biddle, pp. 219–20.

6. Jonathan Elliot, *The American Diplomatic Code,* 2 vols. (Washington, D. C., 1834), I, 524.

to pay, and the Second Bank returned the bill to the United States Treasury with a claim for the usual damages. The Treasury redeemed the bill, but refused to pay the damages. Failing other means of redress, the Bank finally deducted the damages from its semiannual payment to the Treasury in July, 1834. The government then sued the Bank to recover the damages, and it is clear that the Bank could not expect any cooperation or consideration from the government, even when engaged on government business.[7]

The major source of friction concerned drafts on the Second Bank given by the Secretary of the Treasury to several banks holding government deposits. These banks feared retaliatory measures by the Second Bank, and the drafts were for their protection. Contrary to normal practice, however, the Second Bank was not notified of their existence and so could not provide for their payment. Under the best of circumstances these drafts would pose a source of friction. But the banks receiving them did not wait until they were needed in the normal course of business. Either they cashed them immediately, or they expanded their business to the point where they needed the cash to avoid insolvency. The Second Bank thus was called upon to pay $200,000 to the Union Bank of Maryland on October 5, 1833, $500,000 to the Girard Bank of Philadelphia on November 2, and $500,000 to the Manhattan Bank of New York on November 18.[8] These were not inconsiderable sums; they represented about one quarter of the government's deposits with the Second Bank.

Given these and other provocations, the Bank curtailed its operations. The date of the curtailment is usually given as the year starting in August, 1833.[9] This period encompassed the orders given by Biddle for the curtailment, and it therefore

7. Catterall, pp. 299–302. Catterall added (p. 302), "that the nation's honor was forfeit by the refusal to pay the damages. On precisely the same plea it might have refused to pay the principal and interest."
8. Catterall, pp. 302–04.
9. *Ibid.*, p. 314; Smith, pp. 160–65; Jacob P. Meerman, "The Climax of the Bank War: Biddle's Contraction, 1833–34," *Journal of Political Economy*, LXXI (August, 1963), 378–88.

shows the process of contraction, that is, the period in which the Second Bank decreased its operations. It follows that the Bank's activities were low after the contraction had taken effect. A look at Table 3.1 below will make this clear. The liquid assets of the Second Bank began to fall in the third quarter of 1833, when the curtailment began. But they were low all through

TABLE 3.1

Discounts and Domestic Exchange
of the Second Bank, 1832–35 (*millions of dollars*)

	1832	1833	1834	1835
January 1		61.6	54.9	51.8
April 1		64.3	54.8	61.9
July 1		63.3	51.0	65.1
October 1	63.6	60.0	46.0	

SOURCE: *Catterall, p. 325n.*

1834, reaching their low point after the curtailment was "over." The main political controversy was in 1833, but the economic consequences came in 1834.

As the Second Bank curtailed its activities, it forced others to do so also. People who had been accustomed to borrowing from the Second Bank found that they could not do so. They therefore could not lend to those they normally loaned to. The price of borrowed money—the discount rate—rose and remained "high and variable" throughout 1834.[10] But the pressure was not as great as it had been in 1819 or as it would be in 1837. There was comparatively little panic, and banks did not refuse to redeem their notes in specie. As a result, we may assume—although we do not have the data to confirm our expectation—that the effects on the rest of the economy were not strong.[11]

10. Walter Buckingham Smith and Arthur Harrison Cole, *Fluctuations in American Business, 1790–1860* (Cambridge: Harvard University Press, 1935), p. 192.
11. Meerman collected most of the available systematic data; it is almost exclusively about monetary matters. We know little about employment or production in 1834.

Why didn't the contraction become a panic? Either the financial community was not very frightened by the contraction, or the contraction itself did not decrease the availability of bank reserves. Stated differently, the demand for specie may have been smaller than in other crises or the supply of specie may have been larger. It is hard to measure the intensity of the demand, but we know that there was a large increase in the supply of specie during 1834. In the absence of other information on this matter, we therefore attribute the mildness of the contraction of 1834 to the unusually large supply of specie available in that year.

This conclusion is important only if we can discover the source of the specie and use the distinction between supply and demand to investigate further the events of 1834. To know why there was no panic in 1834, we have to know where the specie came from.

The essence of the contraction was the scarcity of credit. Discount rates on commercial paper in Boston and New York were "high and variable" in 1834, and business was unsettled as a result. Since the contraction was a specifically American phenomenon, the rise in American discount rates was not echoed by a rise in English rates. There consequently was a clear incentive for the employment of English mercantile capital in the United States, and capital was exported from Britain for that purpose. As this capital movement was not accompanied by a movement of goods—indeed the American demand for imports was lower than usual because of the contraction—Americans found themselves with an excess of foreign exchange. The price of the pound fell to the point where it became profitable to buy specie in preference to waiting to buy commodities. The result was an unprecedented inflow of specie into the United States. Seventeen million dollars in specie were imported in fiscal 1834 (the year ending August 31, 1834), of which slightly less than half was the result of the process just described.[12]

12. See Smith and Cole, p. 192, and Matthews, p. 201, for the relevant discount rates. Capital imports were large in 1834, but not out

A little background is necessary to justify this quantitative statement, and we digress a bit to explain more about the international exchange. The value of the British pound was fixed in terms of gold, as was the value of the American dollar, and the value of the pound was thus fixed in terms of the dollar by the relative value of the gold in each. The gold in a pound was worth $4.65, and we can term this rate of exchange "gold par." [13]

If the facts just given were the only relevant ones, we would expect the gold par to be the equilibrium exchange rate. If the price of pounds in dollars were less than this rate, it could be profitable to buy pounds with dollars, sell the pounds in Britain for gold at the official rate, ship the gold to the United States and sell the gold to the American government for dollars at the official American rate. The gain would come from the discrepancy between the direct exchange rate of dollars for pounds and the indirect exchange rate through gold (gold par). Not all of this gain would be profit—the gold had to be shipped from Britain to the United States—but if the discrepancy between the exchange rate and gold par exceeded the cost of shipping and insuring gold, gold would flow until the price of foreign exchange had risen to eliminate the profit. Since the transportation cost for specie was about 2 or 3 percent of its value, the exchange rate would not stay below a 2 or 3 percent discount from gold par.[14] The same argument in reverse shows why the exchange rate could not exceed a 2 or 3 percent premium over gold par for very long.

Unhappily for the relevance of this textbook example, the value of the dollar was fixed in silver as well as in gold, and it

of line with succeeding years. Exports were rising rapidly, however, and the failure of imports to keep pace produced the resulting surplus of foreign exchange. See Douglass C. North, "The United States Balance of Payments, 1790–1860," in *Trends in the American Economy in the Nineteenth Century,* Studies in Income Wealth, Vol. 24 (Princeton: Princeton University Press for the National Bureau of Economic Research, 1960), pp. 605; 621.

13. It was 2.7 percent above the official par of $4.44.
14. Myers, I, 74–75; Macesich, 1960, p. 416n.

was worth 15 times as much silver as gold. The pound was not valued in terms of silver, but there was a market for silver in London. The price of silver in pounds can be converted into an exchange rate between silver and gold by expressing the value of the pound in gold at the official rate; the price of gold was 15.7 times the price of silver in London in the early 1830's.[15]

Gold thus could buy 5 percent more silver in London than in the United States. As a result, no one would go through the transaction just described. The exchange dealer would buy silver instead of gold in the London market, ship the silver to the United States and sell the silver to the United States Treasury for dollars. He would earn an extra 5 percent on his transactions by this change.

In fact, the exchange dealer could earn money by shipping silver even when the exchange rate was at gold par, since his gross profit (5 percent) would outweigh his expenses (2 or 3 percent). At this exchange rate there would be a flow of pounds to Britain in return for silver flowing to the United States. Equilibrium was the rate at which the flow of silver—not the less profitable flow of gold—would not be profitable. This rate was 5 percent above the gold par in fiscal 1834.[16]

Did the exchange rate fall far enough below the equilibrium exchange rate to induce an inflow of silver during 1834? We cannot observe the exchange rate directly, as there were no quotations of the rate alone. The quotations were the prices of bills of exchange, and these bills combined an exchange function and a credit function. The price thus represented not the price of pounds, but the price of pounds less the cost of a loan

15. J. Lawrence Laughlin, *The History of Bimetallism in the United States,* 4th Ed. (New York, 1897), pp. 61, 288–91.

16. Davis and Hughes miss this point in their helpful article. They convert their quotations from official par to gold par, but not to the equilibrium rate before 1834. Their conversion, however, appears to contain an arithmetic error. The exchange rate could stay this far above gold par because there was no gold left in the United States to send abroad. Lance E. Davis and Jonathan R. T. Hughes, "A Dollar-Sterling Exchange, 1803–1895," *Economic History Review,* Second Series, XIII (August, 1960), 52–78.

for the duration of the bill. (It will be recalled from Chapter 2 that the interest charge for the loan was deducted from the amount of the loan when the bill was discounted.) The price of bills on London was thus below the exchange rate by the interest charge, which can be measured by the discount rate and which was between 1 and 4 percent for 60-day bills.[17]

The price of 60-day bills on London remained well above the gold par between dollars and pounds in the years before 1834. In that year, the price of 60-day bills fell below gold par to a low point of 4 percent discount from gold par in February.[18] At this price, it was profitable to buy bills on London, buy silver—or even gold at this price—and ship it to the United States for exchange into dollars. The opportunity was not missed, and $8 million in specie was imported from Britain and France in fiscal 1834.[19] Out of a total specie import of $17 million, almost half was due to the low price of foreign exchange. The Second Bank's contraction thus had the paradoxical effect of increasing the specie reserves of the country.[20]

The contraction of 1834 was mild, therefore, because banks were able to accumulate specie without markedly decreasing their loans. The mechanism was simple: As banks attempted to protect themselves by decreasing their liabilities, credit became hard to obtain. English capital flowed in to fill the void, creating an excess supply of foreign exchange and causing its price to fall. When the price of foreign exchange fell far enough, specie was imported, enabling the banks to strengthen their position by increasing their reserves instead of decreasing their liabilities.

17. The rate for 60 days is the annual rate divided by 6.
18. Smith and Cole, p. 190. Davis and Hughes' data (Table A–4) show a fall to almost 10 percent below nominal par, which was below gold par.
19. Two million came from France, and three million was in gold. We have assumed that the exchange with France moved with the exchange on Britain. See Table 3.5, p. 81.
20. Meerman asserted, p. 387, that "through coincidence, foreign commerce was unusually favorable in providing an 'antidote' to the contraction." The examination of exchange rates just presented shows that the antidote was hardly coincidental.

The contraction was therefore mild, but the added specie remained in the system, providing an inflationary element when the banks returned to their normal practice.

Monetary Causes of the Inflation

Inflation, of course, was the dominant economic fact of the 1830's. Prices rose by 50 percent in the three years following 1834, producing—according to most versions—the crisis that followed. This inflation has been characterized as "a period of unparalleled speculation" and "an orgy of spending and speculation" by the authors of standard American history texts.[21] These are emotional terms embodying moral judgments. Historians apparently believe there was something wrong with the price rise of the 1830's, that it resulted from the excesses of evil men. Let us re-examine the record to see if this view can be substantiated.

There are several price indexes that could be used to give an idea of the inflation, and we have selected Smith and Cole's index for use here. It was designed to show "the tone of business in the northeastern section of the country," but comparison with other regional indexes show that the price movements were national in scope.[22] The prices are presented in Table 3.2, where the following pattern emerges. Prices had drifted downward through the 1820's (with a small upward deviation from the trend in the boomlet of 1825) to a trough in the summer of 1830. They then rose about 20 percent in the next three years, peaking at the end of 1833. As a result of the contraction just described, prices fell to a new trough in the second quarter of 1834 at a level only about 5 percent above

21. Morison and Commager, p. 486; Williams, Current and Friedel, I, 385. Hughes and Rosenberg chronicle similar phrases by economic historians.
22. Smith and Cole, p. 157. Other price indexes are presented in Arthur Harrison Cole, *Wholesale Commodity Prices in the United States, 1700–1861,* 2 vols. (Cambridge: Harvard University Press, 1938) and graphed in Macesich, 1960.

TABLE 3.2

Index of Wholesale Commodity Prices: Monthly, 1825–45
(Base: 1834–42)

	JAN.	FEB.	MARCH	APRIL	MAY	JUNE	JULY	AUG.	SEPT.	OCT.	NOV.	DEC.
1825	100	100	104	114	115	117	113	110	107	109	105	106
1826	103	103	98	97	94	93	95	92	90	92	94	93
1827	94	95	95	95	92	91	89	90	91	91	92	94
1828	88	90	88	88	87	88	88	88	89	91	91	95
1829	95	94	93	92	89	89	85	85	85	85	86	85
1830	85	84	84	82	84	83	82	83	85	87	88	88
1831	86	88	89	90	89	90	87	87	89	91	92	91
1832	96	93	92	90	90	90	88	88	88	90	92	93
1833	94	91	92	91	93	93	93	96	98	99	98	98
1834	94	91	88	86	87	87	88	89	92	93	94	97
1835	99	98	100	103	107	110	115	115	113	111	112	116
1836	118	116	121	128	122	118	116	119	122	128	130	127
1837	128	131	129	119	102	102	103	103	98	101	106	108
1838	107	103	101	100	100	101	102	102	107	113	115	117
1839	118	125	124	123	120	118	114	112	112	108	104	101
1840	92	93	90	85	84	82	81	82	86	89	90	89
1841	88	90	88	87	88	84	84	86	91	90	87	85
1842	84	80	78	75	74	73	73	72	70	69	68	69
1843	69	67	67	68	70	71	72	73	74	73	74	73
1844	74	75	75	76	74	73	72	73	72	73	74	74
1845	72	72	74	78	78	76	76	77	79	78	83	86

SOURCE: *Smith and Cole, p. 158.*

the trough in 1830. Prices rose rapidly from this new trough and reached a peak level 50 percent above it during the first quarter of 1837. They then fell irregularly from this peak to a new trough in 1843 about 20 percent below the low points in 1830 or 1834.

One can view these data either as describing an inflation lasting from 1830 to 1837 with a temporary interruption in 1834 or as describing a combination of a mild inflation before 1833 followed by an independent, sharper price rise from 1834 to 1837. The difference between these two views is that the former assumes a single cause behind the price rises of the 1830's, while the latter sees the price rise after 1834 as the result of factors different from those causing the earlier rise. The latter is the traditional view; we look now at the reasoning behind it.

The starting point is Biddle's statement, given above, that the Bank of the United States was no longer responsible for the currency after 1834. The Second Bank, it will be recalled, exerted a policing function on state banks by presenting their notes for redemption. Released from constraint, the state banks are supposed to have expanded their earning assets and their monetary liabilities. And according to the traditional account one method of doing this was favored above all others. Men contracted bank loans in order to buy land from the government, paying for the land with bank notes. The government did not deposit its receipts in the Second Bank after 1834; it placed them in local deposit banks. Deposit banks, viewing the government deposits as reserves—rather than as the volatile asset that the bank notes of other banks actually were—issued more loans. These loans were used to buy more land, and the process repeated itself. In other words, so the story goes, government deposits were considered to be reserves by the deposit banks, and these "reserves" could be acquired by issuing more loans. The stock of money increased rapidly, and a major land boom developed.[23]

This is a plausible line of reasoning, and it was used by contemporary observers as well as later historians.[24] It provides a reason for the price rise after 1834 that could not have been present before the bank war. And—more importantly—it shows how political decisions can affect the economy. But plausibility is not accuracy, and the data must be questioned a bit more closely before this view is accepted. If it is correct, we should find three things. First, since bank expansion is supposed to have caused the inflation, the supply of money should have

23. See Bourne, p. 15, as quoted in Chapter 1, above, and the sources cited there.

24. See Nathan Appleton, *Remarks on Currency and Banking* (Boston, 1841), p. 50; Hammond, pp. 452–53.

risen with the price level. Second, since banks expanded by treating government deposits as reserves, the supply of money should have risen because the true reserve ratio of banks fell—that is, because banks utilized their new freedom to expand their notes and deposits without increasing their specie reserves. And third, since the land boom giving rise to increased government deposits was in the West and South, the reserve ratio of Western and Southern banks should have fallen most rapidly.

The relevant data are presented in Table 3.3 below. These data are basic to our narrative, and their derivation is

TABLE 3.3

The Supply of Money and Its Determinants, 1820–39

END OF YEAR	MONEY	SPECIE	RESERVE RATIO	PROPORTIONS OF MONEY HELD AS SPECIE
	($ million)	($ million)	(percent)	(percent)
1820	85	41	32	24
1821	96	39	30	16
1822	81	32	21	23
1823	88	31	25	15
1824	88	32	27	13
1825	106	29	19	10
1826	108	32	20	12
1827	101	32	20	14
1828	114	31	18	11
1829	105	33	22	12
1830	114	32	23	6
1831	155	30	15	5
1832	150	31	16	5
1833	168	41	18	8
1834	172	51	27	4
1835	246	65	18	10
1836	276	73	16	13
1837	232	88	20	23
1838	240	87	23	18
1839	215	83	20	23

SOURCES: *See Appendix.*

extremely important. Since this derivation is a bit complex, however, it has been relegated to an Appendix.[25]

Table 3.3 presents estimates of the money supply together with the determinants of it isolated by Friedman and Schwartz.[26] Since bank notes and deposits were promises to pay specie on demand, the reserves of banks consisted of the amount of specie they could command, and the amount of specie in the country was an important determinant of the supply of money. If the amount of specie in the country doubled while the other two determinants of the money supply remained constant, the reserves in the system would double, and the quantity of money would also. But we cannot assume that the other determinants of the money supply stayed constant. Banks did not maintain a fixed reserve ratio. They varied the ratio of their specie reserves to their notes and deposits, and this ratio is also an important determinant of the monetary stock. The higher the reserve ratio, the smaller the quantity of money for a given quantity of specie. Finally, the public did not always behave the same. Money— those things that could be used for ordinary transactions— consisted of bank notes, deposits in commercial banks, and coins (that is, specie) in the hands of the public. Part of the specie therefore would be in the hands of the public rather than in the banks. If so, it would not be available to be used as bank reserves, and the quantity of money would be smaller than if it were in banks. The higher the proportion of money the public was willing to hold as bank obligations—that is, the lower the proportion of money held by the public in gold and silver coins—the higher the money supply could be for a given stock of specie and reserve ratio. The three determinants shown in Table 3.3 together uniquely determine the supply of money.[27]

25. The method of presentation does not imply that the derivation of the data is less important than the analysis being presented here; it has been adopted simply in an attempt to keep an already intricate exposition within bounds.

26. Friedman and Schwartz. The determinants in Table 3.3 are simple functions of the ones Friedman and Schwartz used.

27. *Ibid.,* pp. 784–89.

Our first expectation is shown to be fulfilled by the first column of Table 3.3. The quantity of money rose with the price level, reaching a peak at the end of 1836, the closest observation to the price-level peak in the first quarter of 1837. The rise in the quantity of money was also large enough—perhaps even too large—to explain a price rise of 50 percent in the years just before 1837. We may accept, for the moment, the hypothesis that the rise in the supply of money before 1837 caused the rise in prices.

But what caused the money supply to increase? Our second expectation is that the rise was caused by a fall in the reserve ratio. This expectation is *not* fulfilled. The third column of Table 3.3 shows that the reserve ratio of the American banking system as a whole did not fall below its 1831 level throughout the 1830's. Banks were enabled to hold low reserves because the Second Bank of the United States was an effective policeman, not because it had vanished. As discounts on notes decreased in the 1820's, the public increasingly was willing to hold them in place of specie. Notes circulated more widely and returned less often to the issuing bank. Banks could thus hold lower reserves for each dollar of notes or deposits issued, and reserve ratios were low. (The proportion of money held as specie was low also.) A low reserve ratio can be a sign of good banking or of bad banking; in this case it is an indication of the stability of the banking system under the Second Bank.

Having attained this low level, the reserve ratio stayed essentially constant for the next five years; only in 1834 did the reserve ratio deviate sharply from the level reached in 1831, and it never fell below the 1831 level. The data in Table 3.1 showed that the contraction following the removal of the deposits from the Second Bank took place within 1834, although the removal of the deposits occurred in 1833. Accordingly, the effects of the contraction are shown in the observation for late 1834, rather than late 1833 as might have been expected from a reading of the political record alone. In 1834 the banks were well protected, the Second Bank having drawn in its horns to protect itself from the Treasury and to influence the government, and the state banks having contracted as a result of the Second Bank's pressure.

Since the reserve ratio did not fall below its previous level after the removal of the government deposits from the Second Bank, the explanation that sees the "freeing" of the state banks at that time as the genesis of the inflation must be rejected. As the reserve ratio of 1834 was clearly atypical of the years around it, there is also little reason to date the inflation from that year. During the 1820's the stock of money had risen very slowly. The reserve ratio of banks and the proportion of the money stock held by the public as specie had fallen, and these changes expanded the supply of money a little even though the amount of specie in the United States did not rise. This pattern changed in the early 1830's, when the reserve ratio and the proportion of money held as specie reached their nadir, and the amount of specie in the country began to rise. The inflation of the 1830's dates from this turnabout, from 1831 or 1832.

The traditional explanation has not been in accord with the data on the banking system as a whole; let us see if it performs better with less aggregate data. According to this view, the expansion of bank loans was greatest in the regions of land speculation: in the South and West. Even if the banking system as a whole did not reduce its reserve ratio, perhaps the banks in these areas did.

Table 3.4 (opposite) contains the reserve ratios of state banks by region, presented here as they can be derived from two sources. The two sets of data agree remarkably well, considering the difficulties of getting adequate coverage of some 900 state banks, but their differences show clearly the limitations of the data. For example, the Treasury data do not show a change in the reserve ratio of the Southwestern region, while Van Fenstermaker's data show a fall before 1836. Given the constancy of the first observation, it is hard to put much weight on the change in the second; we cannot get too close to the historical reality through these data.

Nevertheless, a few firm conclusions can be drawn from the

data. The reserve ratios of state banks were not lowest in the South and West where the excesses of banking were presumed to have occurred; they were far lower in staid New England. This paradox is resolved by the observation made above, that a low reserve ratio can be a sign either of bad banking or of good banking. In this case, as in the case of the national ratio before

TABLE 3.4

Reserve Ratios of State Banks by Region, 1834–37

END OF YEAR	NEW ENGLAND	MIDDLE ATLANTIC	SOUTH-EAST	SOUTH-WEST	NORTH-WEST
Treasury Data					
1834	.06	.22	.24	.13	.46
1835	.07	.16	.21	.15	.28
1836	.07	.14	.18	.14	.30
1837	.09	.19	.24	.13	.32
Van Fenstermaker's Data					
1834	.10	.21	.26	.21	.39
1835	.11	.16	.25	.17	.27
1836	.10	.18	.20	.13	.31
1837	.12	.26	.24	.13	.36

SOURCES: *See Appendix. Regions were defined as follows:*
New England: Me., N. H., Vt., Mass., R. I., Conn.
Middle Atlantic: N. Y., Pa., N. J., Del., Md., D. C.
Southeast: Va., N. C., S. C., Ga., Fla.
Southwest: La., Ark., Ala., Miss., Tenn., Ky.
Northwest: Wis., Mich., Ill., Ind., O., Mo.

1834, it is the latter. The Suffolk Bank in New England kept funds to redeem the notes of the banks of that region, and the public had confidence that their notes could be redeemed at will. Consequently they did not attempt to redeem them very often, and New England banks could keep lower reserves than banks elsewhere in the country. Clearly, the low reserve ratios of New England banks did not constitute an element of instability in the antebellum banking structure.

The fall in the reserve ratios after 1834 was confined almost entirely to the Middle Atlantic and Northwestern regions. We may infer that the contraction of that year hit those regions most strongly, missing the Southern part of the country and New England. The Second Bank did not do much business in New England, and the Bank's contraction might not have affected banks there, but it is not clear why the contraction did not show up in the data for the South. Of course, if Van Fenstermaker's data are correct, the effects of the contraction can be seen in the reserve ratio of the Southwestern region (which contained New Orleans), with which the Second Bank did a large business.[28]

Except for the fall in some of the ratios after 1834 and for the problematical fall in the Southwestern ratio in 1836, the reserve ratios of the different regions stayed remarkably constant in the years shown. The data are too scarce to permit a comparison with the years before 1834, but there is no evidence of an expansion of state banks in the South or West as a result of the demise of the policing functions of the Second Bank. In fact, the reserve ratios of the Northwestern region were high enough to inspire confidence in the banks of that region, although it is probably true that the banks reported in Table 3.4 were the strongest banks of the region. Not only are the expectations produced by the traditional explanation of the inflation not fulfilled on a national level, they are also not fulfilled on a regional level.[29]

It should be noted that reserves consisted solely of specie

28. Sumner, p. 189; Catterall, p. 135.
29. One could argue along different lines that the removal of the deposits acted to reduce the aggregate reserve ratio by transferring specie from the Bank of the United States to the state banks, since the latter had lower reserve ratios than the former. The Bank of the United States still had one third of the specie in banks in late 1834; it must have acquired substantial parts of the specie inflow of that year. But this proportion fell rapidly over the next two years, and it stabilized at about one tenth in late 1836. This fall helped to reduce the reserve ratio of the banking system as a whole, although the reserve ratio of the state banks alone was above the level sustained from late 1831 through 1833. See the sources for Table 3.3, Appendix.

and that deposits included the Federal Government's surplus. If the banks had treated the government deposits as reserves and expanded on that basis, this expansion would have appeared as a fall in the reserve ratios of Tables 3.3 and 3.4. We may conclude that banks neither saw the removal of the deposits from the Second Bank as a signal for unsupported expansion nor confused government deposits with reserves. In short, the reserve ratio did not fall after 1831.

The willingness of the public to hold bank notes or deposits in place of specie also did not increase. The public held only 5 percent of its money in the form of specie in 1831–32, if the data in Table 3.3 are correct, and they were not willing to reduce this low proportion any more (except in the unusual year 1834). Five percent is a low proportion, and any reader is justified if he questions its accuracy. It is, in fact, lower than the proportion of money held in coin at the start of the 20th century.[30] But while considerable doubt about the level of the specie stock can be justified, the changes in the specie stock are known with more precision. As the Appendix shows, if the estimates of the specie stock used here are replaced by estimates generated by cumulating the effects of foreign trade and domestic mining, the results for the 1830's are not changed. Consequently, we may assert with confidence that an increased willingness of the public to hold bank obligations in place of specie was *not* an inflationary factor in the 1830's, although we may remain skeptical that their willingness had attained the remarkable heights at the start of the 1830's shown in Table 3.3.

The factor leading to an expansion of the monetary stock, then, was the rise in the stock of specie. The amount of specie in the country more than doubled in the quinquennium following 1832.[31] No matter what Jackson had done to or for the

30. U. S. Bureau of the Census, *Historical Statistics of the United States, Colonial Times to 1957* (Washington, D. C., 1960), pp. 646–48.

31. Of course, if the specie stock was larger than shown in Table 3.3, its rise was proportionately less. Any reasonable adjustment, how-

Second Bank, this increase in the specie stock would have led to a large increase in the stock of money. In a monetary system based on specie reserves, an increase in these reserves—unless opposed by conscious actions only dreamed of in the 20th century—can have no other effect.

The importance of this change in the specie stock cannot be overestimated. It completely shatters the link between Jackson's actions and the inflation assumed by most historians, and it starts us on the road to a new view of the interaction of political and economic actions in the 1830's.

But what caused the stock of specie to rise? If this change can be shown to have been the result of Jackson's actions, then a new link between the Bank War and the inflation will have been found. If, on the other hand, the specie stock rose for reasons unconnected with the Bank War, the inflation cannot be seen as its result. We have already seen that a substantial part of the increase in specie in 1834 can be attributed to the low price of foreign exchange due to the contraction instituted as part of the Bank War. To this extent, the Bank War produced the inflation; what about the far larger part of the rise in the supply of specie still to be explained?

Macesich has argued that the entire increase in the specie stock could be accounted for by factors similar to those affecting the change in 1834. He said that an excess supply of foreign exchange forced the price of foreign exchange down to the point where it was profitable to import specie, not just for 1834 but for the whole inflationary period.[32] The problems of verifying such a view for 1834 have been discussed. For the later years, there are more problems. As part of his campaign against banks, Jackson supported a proposal to raise the price of gold in the United States in order to attract gold from Europe and to induce the public to use gold instead of bank obligations for their business. This proposal passed Congress, and on August 1,

---

ever, still leaves an enormous rise. See the Appendix for contemporary estimates of the specie in the United States.

32. Macesich, 1960, especially p. 413.

1834, the official price of gold in the United States was raised from 15 to 16 times the price of silver. The price of gold in terms of silver in the United States became slightly higher than the price in England, and it was more profitable to import gold than silver into the United States as a result.[33] Consequently, the gold par between pounds and dollars became the equilibrium rate, and only when the exchange rate fell below the gold par minus the cost of shipping was it profitable to ship gold to the United States in return for the shipment of bills in the opposite direction. Turning to the data, we find that in addition to the data on bills of exchange used before, there are estimates of the exchange rate for 1835 and later years derived by adding the interest charge to the price of bills. Neither set of data indicates that the pound was undervalued enough to induce a flow of specie in any year except 1834.[34]

Macesich's explanation fails fundamentally because it looks in the wrong place for the sources of the specie. The specie stock rose because of specie imports, but most of the imports were not from Europe. Table 3.5 shows the imports of specie for the 1830's, broken down by country of origin and by the metal involved.[35] Only in three years during the 1830's were there imports of specie from Europe. The inflow from Europe in 1834 has already been discussed. The inflow in 1836 represented the payment of the French indemnity that had been controversial in 1833.[36] And the inflow in 1838 came after the inflation had ended. Most of the specie had to come for reasons other than the undervaluation of the pound.

33. The aim of the change was to encourage the importation of gold. Thomas Hart Benton, *Thirty Years' View,* 2 vols. (New York, 1854), I, 440; Laughlin, Chapter 4.
34. Smith and Cole, p. 190; Davis and Hughes. Davis and Hughes' series for the exchange rate start only in 1835; before that they present bill prices.
35. The yearly totals do not match exactly the changes in the specie stock shown in Table 3.3, but over the decade they are very close. The discrepancies are discussed in detail in the Appendix.
36. U. S. Congress, Senate Document 351, 25th Congress, 2nd Session (1837–38), pp. 124–25.

The source of the specie is apparent from Table 3.5. Most of it came from Mexico, with imports from various Latin American countries adding to the flow.[37] In the 1820's, the inflow of silver from Mexico and Latin America was offset by an outflow to Asia. This balance was destroyed in the 1830's by a small rise in the imports from Mexico and a larger fall in the specie exports to China.

Silver was a commodity export for Mexico, and the increase in its quantity during the mid-1830's was probably due to an increase in supply. The price of silver was fixed in terms of American currency, and the American inflation reduced the quantity of goods bought by a unit of silver. Consequently, the added imports from Mexico were not produced by offers of higher prices for them.[38]

The decline in the exports of silver to China and Asia was large enough to make the annual amount of silver retained from the Mexican imports rise from a very small amount in the late 1820's to about $4 million in the 1830's, contributing about $20 million of silver to the American stock of specie between 1831 and 1836. The Chinese were increasing their consumption of opium in the 1830's, and they abandoned their traditional desire for silver in favor of a demand for bills on London to buy opium from British India.

The story, of course, is a little more complex than this. The United States had a continual trade deficit with China, which was covered in the 1820's by shipments of Mexican silver. The Chinese were buying over $10 million worth of opium a year from the British during the 1830's, and they were paying for it partly by merchandise exports, but mainly with silver. American

37. The inflow from Mexico was almost entirely in specie (coin) rather than bullion, as Mexican coins were legal tender in the United States. See Arthur Nussbaum, *A History of the Dollar* (New York: Columbia University Press, 1957), pp. 56, 62, 84; and Sources for Table 3.5.

38. "Silver is imported directly from Mexico and other parts of America, of which it is the natural product, and must, as the cotton of the United States, be necessarily exported annually, without regard to price or rate of exchange." Gallatin, p. 65.

TABLE 3.5

Net Imports (−) of Gold and Silver by Country
of Origin, 1825–39 (millions of dollars)

FISCAL YEAR		ENGLAND	FRANCE	MEXICO	ASIA	OTHER *	TOTAL
1825	Gold	...	...	...	...	...	...
	Silver	...	1	−3	6	−1	3
1826	Gold	...	...	...	...	...	...
	Silver	1	...	−3	3	−4	−3
1827	Gold	...	...	...	...	...	...
	Silver	...	2	−4	4	−3	−1
1828	Gold	...	...	...	...	...	...
	Silver	2	2	−4	2	−2	...
1829	Gold	...	...	...	...	...	...
	Silver	...	2	−4	1	−2	−3
1830	Gold	...	...	...	...	...	...
	Silver	...	...	−5	...	−2	−7
1831	Gold	...	...	...	...	...	...
	Silver	2	3	−4	1	−2	...
1832	Gold	...	...	...	...	...	...
	Silver	1	...	−4	2	−1	−2
1833	Gold	...	...	...	...	...	...
	Silver	...	...	−5	1	−1	−5
1834	Gold	−2	−1	...	...	−1	−4
	Silver	−4	−1	−7	1	−2	−13
1835	Gold	−1	−1	...	...	...	−2
	Silver	...	1	−8	3	−2	−6
1836	Gold	−2	−4	...	...	−1	−7
	Silver	...	...	−4	2	−1	−3
1837	Gold	1	−1	...	...	−1	−1
	Silver	1	1	−5	1	−3	−5
1838	Gold	−9	−1	...	...	−1	−11
	Silver	−1	...	−3	1	−1	−4
1839	Gold	2	...	...	...	...	2
	Silver	−1	1	−2	2	...	...

* Primarily Latin America.
SOURCES: See Appendix, particularly Table A.3.
[Imports of specie appear in the table with a negative sign because they
are deficit items in conventional balance-of-payments accounting. They
use foreign exchange; they do not earn it.]

merchants could have continued to transport silver to China for the Chinese to sell to the British, but this would have necessitated needlessly sending the silver around the world. It was much more efficient for the American merchant to send a bill on London to the Orient. He could then buy opium from the English merchant with the bill and Chinese goods with the opium. The Chinese would not need to worry about complicated international financial transactions, and the Western merchants would not have to send silver back and forth.[39]

This practice appears to have been adopted. The Bank of the United States encouraged it by introducing long-dated bills of exchange (the China or India bills) specially for the Eastern trade.[40] It would not be too misleading to say that the Opium War was more closely connected to the American inflation than the Bank War between Jackson and Biddle.

Other Causes of the Inflation

The movements of specie were dramatic and apparent. Yet an account of specie movements does not tell the whole story. In particular, three questions that were glossed over in the preceding section deserve attention. First, why did the increase in the supply of money lead to an increase in prices? Second, why did not this rise in prices lead to a specie flow *from* the United

39. The Chinese had a trade surplus of about $3 million with England, but they were buying between 10 and 15 million dollars' worth of opium a year. The recorded shipments of silver to England were on the order of 6 to 8 million dollars annually, but they may have been even larger to cover the Chinese purchases of opium. A British observer said: "The drain of silver for opium has, without a doubt, checked our trade between England and China, and by impoverishing the Chinese, it has prevented the sale of our manufactures." R. Montgomery Martin, *China: Political, Commercial and Social; in an Official Report to Her Majesty's Government* (London, 1847), I, 148, 176; and also Samuel Eliot Morison, *The Maritime History of Massachusetts, 1783–1860* (Boston: Houghton Mifflin [Sentry Edition], 1961), p. 277; and John King Fairbank, *Trade and Diplomacy on the China Coast* (Cambridge: Harvard University Press, 1953), I, 63–78.
40. Catterall, p. 112; Sumner, pp. 189–90; Smith, pp. 34, 89.

States *to* Europe? And third, what was the actual relationship between the inflation and the land boom of the 1830's?

There is no necessary connection between money and prices, and there are several possible outcomes to a rise in the supply of money. As the money supply increased, people attempted to spend their increased monetary holdings, and the effects of these attempts depended both on what they wanted to buy and how the economy was operating.

For instance, people might have tried to purchase bonds or other financial securities with the money. This would have raised the price of the desired securities and lowered their yield. And as the interest rate fell, the inducement to buy them would have waned. People would have been content to hold more money than before—because the desired alternative was no longer as attractive—and the principal effect of the rise in the supply of money would have been to lower the interest rate. This possibility, however, is of theoretical interest only, for it is hard to find a consistent pattern in the movement of interest rates during the 1830's. The short-term interest rate fluctuated wildly, but reached high levels only in or near financial panics. The long-term rate scarcely moved at all.[41] The interest rate cannot be said to have fallen in the 1830's.

Rather than buy securities, people tried to buy goods and services with their newly acquired money. This could have had either of two effects (or a combination of both): the production of goods and services might have risen to meet the increased demand, or—if this was not possible—the rise in demand would have raised prices.

It seems quite likely that production did rise during the boom of the 1830's. Great public excitement had been generated by the completion and outstanding success of the Erie Canal. Imitations of the Erie Canal, extensions of canals into

41. Smith and Cole, pp. 192–93; Sidney Homer, *A History of Interest Rates* (New Brunswick, N. J.: Rutgers University Press, 1963), pp. 286–87; B. U. Ratchford, *American State Debts* (Durham, N. C.: Duke University Press, 1941), p. 95.

new territories, and railroads to compete with the canals were all getting underway at the time prices started to rise. These construction efforts have received a great deal of attention from historians—as they did from contemporaries—because of their inherent drama and their promise for the future. But construction in the 1830's was still a minor part of the economy, and the expansion of this sector did not have the capacity to equal the expansion in the stock of money. At its peak for the decade in 1839, construction comprised only 10 percent of the gross national product, and railroad and canal construction each composed only about 10 percent of construction—that is, about one percent of the national product.[42] Investment in transportation facilities was even smaller before the 1830's, and its expansion could not raise production as fast as the stock of money rose. The money supply could double in the first half of the 1830's; the national product could not.

In addition to the investment done by Americans, Europeans were investing in the United States. This capital inflow allowed the United States to import more than it exported—that is, to consume more than it produced. Money was needed for the purchase and resale of these imports, but again the import surpluses were too small to account for the increase in the stock of money. Capital imports reached a peak of 5 percent of the national product in 1836; they were smaller as a proportion of income in all other years in the 1830's.[43] Although important for other reasons, the capital imports were not of the same scale as the increase in the stock of money.

Since there were only a few more goods to buy, people

42. The year in question is the year ending May 31, 1839, which is close to the fiscal year ending August 31, 1839. Robert E. Gallman, private correspondence.

43. *Ibid.;* Robert E. Gallman, "Gross National Product in the United States, 1834–1909," in *Output, Employment, and Productivity in the United States after 1800.* Studies in Income and Wealth, Vol. 30 (New York: Columbia University Press for the National Bureau of Economic Research, 1966), p. 15.

attempted to spend the greatly increased stock of money on approximately the same volume of goods. The price of goods rose as a result. Our previous assertion that the changes in the supply of money produced changes in prices therefore can be accepted.

But as prices rose in the United States faster than they rose in other countries, the incentives for foreigners to buy American exports declined, while the incentives for Americans to buy imports rose. The result should have been a deficit in the balance of payments as imports outran exports. It should have been hard to get foreign exchange, the price of foreign exchange should have risen, and specie should have been exported to Europe. The movements of specie can normally be expected to provide a limit to inflation under the kind of monetary system prevailing in the 1830's, and we must ask why the Mexican silver did not just flow through the United States on its way toward a wider diffusion among countries active in international trade. Had it done so, the Chinese would have continued to pay for some of their opium with Mexican silver in the 1830's, but without the transport costs incurred in the 1820's.

The silver did not flow to Europe because the British exported capital to the United States, as was mentioned in connection with the relation of the money supply to prices. The British, in other words, did not ask us to pay for all our imports with goods or specie; they let us owe them for the goods. They had exported capital to South America in the 1820's, but after a lull in all British foreign lending in the late 1820's, British capital exports went primarily to the United States. Measuring from 1827, a year of no British capital exports, to 1837, the capital imports to the United States amounted to three fifths of all capital exports from Britain.[44]

The capital imports were small in relation to our national

44. Albert H. Imlah, *Economic Elements in the Pax Britannica* (Cambridge: Harvard University Press, 1958), pp. 70–71; North, 1960, p. 621.

product, but they were large in relation to the specie flows. The stock of money in the United States was three to five times the stock of specie, depending on the year. The gross national product was about 10 times the stock of money. Consequently the national product was 30 to 50 times the value of the specie in the country, and events too small to affect income could have important repercussions for the stock of specie. The capital inflows were not negligible even compared to the national income—they were 5 percent of the latter at their peak in 1836—and they were certainly large enough to obviate a movement of specie of lesser size from America to Britain.

But why did the British export capital to the United States in this decade? If we can show a connection between the capital inflow and Jackson's policies, we will have found a new link between Jackson and the inflation to replace the old.

If the capital inflow had come solely because of increased American demand, Americans would have had to offer British investors a greater return than at other times to convince them to invest in the United States. Conversely, if the capital inflow had been caused solely by an increased British desire to invest in America, the greater availability of these funds should have forced the return on American investments down below the rates in adjacent decades. As we noted previously, however, the long-term interest rate in this decade was not very different from its level in other decades, and we must conclude that both influences were at work—their effects on the rate of return offsetting each other.[45]

On the American side, there was a demand for capital to build canals and railroads in imitation of and in competition with the Erie Canal and to finance the import surplus resulting from the high prices in America. In Britain, there was an exportable surplus, disillusionment with the direction capital exports had taken in the 1820's—most South American countries

45. The differential between British and American rates was falling over time, and this fall was neither accelerated nor arrested during the 1830's. Homer, pp. 195–96, 286–87.

had already defaulted on their debts—and admiration for the repayment by the United States of its national debt.[46] None of these can be linked with the policy of Jackson's struggle against the Second Bank. Only the last specifically concerns the Federal Government, and it was the result of high tariff revenues rather than any policy toward banks. Explosive tariff controversies had swirled through Jackson's first Administration and been temporarily quieted by the Compromise Tariff of 1833. Unwilling to reopen the tariff question, the government paid off the national debt.[47] The new problems this created will emerge shortly.

We said above that the American inflation was caused by the retention of Mexican silver. We see now that this retention was made possible by capital imports from Britain. The inflation was thus the product of two factors—the change in the Oriental trade and the capital imports from Britain—not just one. It seems unlikely that either could have produced the inflation by itself. As we noted earlier in this section, had the change in Chinese tastes been the only change between the 1820's and 1830's, the Mexican silver would have flowed to Britain. On the other hand, had the British exported as much capital as they did without this change in Chinese tastes having occurred, the inflation would not have developed. Americans did not want to have an import surplus as large as the capital imports at the prices reigning in the 1820's. The price of pounds consequently would have fallen, and specie would have been shipped from Britain to the United States.[48] The specie would have come from the Bank of England's reserves, and the Bank of England would have taken action to retain these reserves. The Bank of

46. Leland H. Jenks, *The Migration of British Capital to 1875* (New York: Knopf, 1927), Chapters 2–3; Sumner, pp. 258–59.

47. Van Deusen, pp. 76–80.

48. This is what Macesich thought had happened. We know that the United States would not have had an import surplus equal to the capital imports of the 1830's at the prices of the 1820's because they had such a surplus in the 1830's when prices in the United States were much higher relative to prices in England than they had been in the 1820's.

England became alarmed at its loss of specie in 1836; had the export of specie to the United States been larger, it would have become alarmed much sooner and put an end to the capital exports to the United States.[49]

When two causes combine to produce a single effect, it is not possible to isolate one or the other as the prime cause. One can as easily say that the capital imports permitted the United States to retain the Mexican silver as that the cessation of silver shipments to China enabled the United States to import capital from Britain. The two events together produced the inflation. Neither of them, it may be repeated, owed anything to the Bank War. The capital imports resulted from the demands of the construction boom stimulated by the success of the Erie Canal and the changeable investing habits of the British. The cessation of silver exports resulted from the introduction of opium into China. Andrew Jackson had no control over these events.

But what about the land boom? The traditional history attributed the expansion of bank credit to the land boom, and we have refuted that view. If banks had made loans on the basis of government deposits, they would have increased the amount of their outstanding notes and deposits faster than they accumulated specie reserves. In other words, their reserve ratios would have fallen. This, as we have seen, did not happen.

Nevertheless, there was a land boom of monumental proportions during the 1830's. Land sales by the Federal Government were under $2 million a year during the 1820's. They rose to about $5 million in 1834 and then jumped to $15 million in 1835 and an almost unbelievable $25 million in 1836. Sales were under $7 million in 1837, and they fell toward their old levels as the boom receded.[50] No rational calculation could

49. See the discussion of the Bank of England's actions in 1836–37 in Chapter 4, below.

50. The acreage figures are only slightly less than the dollar amounts, as the average actual price of land remained close to the official price of $1.25 per acre. *U. S. Historical Statistics,* pp. 239, 712. The dollar figures in *U. S. Historical Statistics* differ slightly from those in Table 4.3 (p. 124).

have produced such a large and brief movement. However the boom started, it was carried away in 1835 and 1836 by speculative fever that did not deign to calculate the expected gains.

Even if we had not already refuted the traditional view of the land boom, the magnitude of the boom would cast doubt on it. The traditional theory implies that the easy availability of credit was the cause of the boom, but could cheaper credit have caused land sales to grow by a factor of five in two years? Either credit must have been very, very cheap in 1835 and 1836, or the elasticity of demand for land must have been very high for this to happen. We know that the cost of capital did not fall to zero. Interest rates in the East show little movement in these years, and Western rates could not have fallen precipitously without having some effect on the East. The traditional theory, therefore, must assert that a small reduction in the cost of land led to a very large increase in the quantity bought—that is, that the price-elasticity of demand was very high.[51]

We do not have data to disprove this hypothesis, but if it is true, the implications for American history are very grave. If a lower price for land would have led many more people to buy land, then the policy of charging high prices for land to raise revenue severely retarded the growth of the country.[52] Consequently, if we do not view the land boom of the 1830's as a speculative movement, but instead attempt to explain it as a rational reaction to changing prices, then we are forced by the magnitudes involved to say that the demand for land was very elastic in the antebellum period and that public land policy markedly slowed the settlement of the country. This may be true, but one would like more evidence before accepting it.

In any case, the land boom acted to *retard* the inflation.

51. Wiltse, p. 256, presented the same proposition in another guise. As prices in the United States rose, public lands that were sold by the government at a fixed price became relatively cheaper. This change in relative price, he asserted, produced the land boom. Obviously he assumed a very high elasticity of demand.

52. I am indebted to William Letwin for directing my attention to this point.

There was a practically unlimited supply of land available to the potential purchaser at a fixed price. For whatever reason, people spent millions of dollars buying this land at a time when the supply of money was increasing rapidly. Money that could have been spent on other things was spent on land and accumulated by the Federal Government.[53] Most other things were available in limited supply, and a greater demand for them would have raised their price. Not so with the public lands; a greater demand increased the quantity sold, but not the price. The demand for land therefore absorbed part of the increased money supply and damped the inflation. Of the $40 million of federal land sales in 1835 and 1836, $34 million have been estimated to have been due to the boom. This equals about one third of the increase in the money supply from late 1834 to late 1836; it was a powerful damping effect during those two years. Far from causing the inflation, the land boom actually retarded it.[54]

Let us summarize the argument so far. The traditional explanation of the inflation laid the blame at the door of the White House. Jackson destroyed the Bank of the United States, freeing other banks to increase the money supply by promoting a land boom and an inflation which fed upon each other. This view is wrong; the money supply increased because the amount of specie in the country increased, not because banks expanded on the basis of fixed reserves. Part of the new specie entered the country as a result of the Bank War and the contraction of 1834, but most came from Mexico and was retained because of changes in the Asian trade. All of it, in a fundamental sense, *stayed* because of the capital imports from England. To a large extent, therefore, the inflation was independent of Jackson's

53. Table 5.3 (p. 168).
54. The analogy with the Keynesian liquidity trap should be clear. The estimate of the "extra" land sales comes from Bourne, pp. 137–38. It is the excess of land sales in 1835 and 1836 over the average of the annual land sales in the decades before and after those years. The money stock increased by about $100 million in these two years; see Table 3.3.

policies. And although the inflation undoubtedly spurred the land boom, the land boom acted to retard the inflation.

The Jacksonians were caught up in a process they did not understand. They encouraged it by their actions, but the story would have been almost the same under a different Administration. If there had not been a contraction in 1834 having the paradoxical effect of increasing the later inflation by drawing specie into the country, there also might not have been the land boom with its unappreciated effect of slowing the price rise. The retention of Mexican silver, and the resultant expansion of the money supply, would have taken place whether or not the Bank of the United States had continued to exist.

The Cotton Market

The discussion has been carried on so far with reference to the economy as a whole. To complete our picture, we need to look more closely at an important part of the economy and to demonstrate the relation between this part and the whole.

Cotton was the single most important commercial commodity to the antebellum economy. It was the largest single crop, accounting for about 20 percent of the value of all crops, and the largest single export, accounting for roughly half of the value of United States exports in the 1830's.[55] Its price was a natural indicator of the well-being of the economy.

It has been asserted, moreover, that the rise in the price of cotton started the speculative boom of the 1830's.[56] The inflation was a natural result of the increasing supply of specie and owed nothing to the cotton market, but the land boom was not.

55. Marvin W. Towne and Wayne D. Rasmussen, "Farm Gross Product and Gross Investment in the Nineteenth Century," in *Trends in the American Economy in the Nineteenth Century.* Studies in Income and Wealth, Vol. 24 (Princeton: Princeton University Press for the National Bureau of Economic Research, 1960), p. 292; *U. S. Historical Statistics,* p. 547.

56. "The rise in cotton prices was the spark which set the fire alight." Matthews, p. 52.

The price of cotton *doubled* in the 1830's; had it continued to rise at the same rate—or even had it continued to rise at all— anyone holding land suitable for growing cotton would have been rich. In 1835 and 1836, people believed that some such trend was developing and they valued land accordingly. Land values rose dramatically, and people rushed to buy more. A land boom was the result.[57]

The land boom acted to retard the inflation, and the rise in cotton prices therefore had the paradoxical result of slowing the rise in other prices. The connection between the land boom and the rise in cotton prices, which is usually presented to show the inflationary effects of the rising cotton price, in fact shows the exact opposite. Since the supply of money rose because the supply of specie rose, not because of unsupported bank expansion, the impact of other factors was often not in the direction usually assumed.

But the rise in cotton prices also had other effects, and these effects acted to increase the inflation. To see what they were, we must examine the causes of the price rise.

The price of cotton at New Orleans, which had been 10 cents or less per pound since 1826, reached a low point near 8 cents a pound in the spring of 1831. It rose slowly for the next two years, and then jumped up dramatically in the fall of 1833. It returned to about 10 cents a pound in the spring of 1834, but was above 15 cents by the year's end. The monthly average did not fall below 14 cents thereafter until the start of 1837, and it was over 17 cents in many months.[58]

It has been common to see the rise in the price of cotton as part of the general price rise, even though this important price rose slightly earlier and rather higher than prices in general, but this is not the only view that can be taken. There are three possible hypotheses that might explain this price rise: First, there might have been a temporary rise in the demand for cot-

57. Lewis Cecil Gray, *History of Agriculture in the Southern United States* (Washington: The Carnegie Institution, 1933), II, 899.
58. *Ibid.*, p. 1027. See Table 3.6, p. 103, for annual averages.

ton. More precisely, since the demand for cotton was growing rapidly throughout the early 19th century, there might have been a more than usually rapid rise in the demand for cotton in the mid-1830's. Second, the United States might have temporarily exhausted its cotton-growing capacity around 1833. And third, the increase in the supply of money could have caused the price of cotton to rise without any pressure on supply or demand in real terms.[59]

The argument behind the third hypothesis assumes that all relevant prices rose, so that the rise in the cotton price was not a change in relative prices. But four fifths of the cotton crop was regularly exported in the 1830's, primarily to Britain.[60] Unless the foreign textile producers were producing for the American market, they would have found their costs rising while the prices at which they could sell their products did not. Britain was the only country that exported cotton textiles to the United States at this time, and less than 10 percent of British cotton-textile exports—and a correspondingly lower share of British cotton-textile production—went to the United States in the 1830's.[61] Consequently, had the price of cotton risen because of the American inflation, it would have had the same effect on the buyers of this cotton as a price rise due to an exhaustion of cotton-growing capacity, and we may discuss the two hypotheses together.

Douglass C. North has argued forcefully for the exhaustion of cotton-growing capacity in the early 1830's. His argument starts from the land booms that swept the country in the years just before 1820, in the 1830's, and in the 1850's. In his words:

During each period of expansion, millions of acres of new land were purchased from the government for cotton production. Once this land had been cleared and a crop or two of corn planted to

59. These are the hypotheses listed by Matthews, pp. 52–53.
60. See Table 3.6, p. 103.
61. J. Potter, "Atlantic Economy, 1815–60: The U. S. A. and the Industrial Revolution in Britain," in L. S. Pressnell (ed.), *Studies in the Industrial Revolution* (London: University of London Press, 1960), p. 258.

prepare the soil, the amount of cotton available could be substantially increased, and the supply curve of cotton shifted very sharply to the right. With the depressed cotton prices that followed such expansion, a good deal of this land was devoted to alternative use. . . . The result is that the supply curve of cotton . . . was highly elastic over a range of output which included all the available land that had been cleared and readied for crop production and was suitable for cotton. . . . When the growth of demand for cotton finally brought all this potential capacity into production, a further increase in demand resulted in substantial price increases as the supply curve became increasingly inelastic.[62]

It will be helpful to restate this argument in terms of a graph (as North did). Figure 1 has been drawn with the quantity of cotton grown in any one year on the horizontal axis and the price of cotton (in that same year) on the vertical axis. The curve marked "S" is the supply curve that North describes as being in existence at the start of the 1830's. The flat part of this supply curve expresses the hypothesis that the quantity of cotton grown could be increased without raising its price up to some point (near Q_3) where the supply of prepared cotton-growing land ran out. In the language of the economist, the supply curve was very elastic over this range. When the supply of land already prepared for growing cotton had been exhausted, it was necessary to prepare new land to increase the size of the cotton crop. This could not be done immediately, and it was necessary to offer a higher price for cotton to induce plantation owners to undertake these preparations or to use existing land more intensively than normal. The supply curve expresses this phenomenon by turning upward—that is, by becoming inelastic.

The point at which the supply curve turned upward was set during each of the antebellum land booms. In each boom, new land was made ready for cotton, and little incentive was needed to induce people to use this new land for that purpose. In terms of Figure 1, each land boom moved the point at which the supply curve turned upward to the right. Between land booms,

62. North, 1961, pp. 71–73.

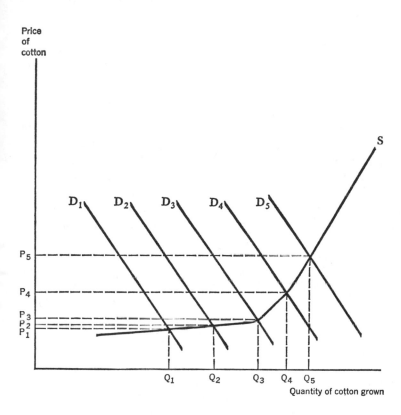

FIGURE 1   Hypothetical Supply and Demand
Curves for Cotton, I

this hypothesis implies that the supply curve did not change, or
at least that very little new land was prepared for cotton.

By asserting that the land purchased during the great land
booms was immediately prepared for cultivation, North's theory
conflicts with the traditional view of the land booms, which
represents the purchases during the booms largely as speculative

ventures—that is, as purchases for resale. The traditional view can be shown to be the correct one in this case.

Land sales were less than 5 million acres in any one year before 1835. They rose to 13 million acres in 1835 and 20 million acres in 1836. They fell to 6 million acres in 1837 and remained below 5 million acres for the next 16 years.[63] We can assert with confidence that all of the land sold in 1835 and 1836 could not have been brought into cultivation immediately. It required 33 man-days on average to clear an acre of land in the 1850's. The costs were roughly the same in the 1830's— neither prices nor technology had changed much in the interim —and it would have required 660 million man-days to clear the land sold by the Federal Government in 1836. The number of people ten and older engaged in farming in 1840 was about 3.6 million. The labor force in 1836 was only slightly less than this; therefore it would have taken about 200 days' work from *everyone* engaged in farming to have cleared all the land sold in 1836. If all of this time had been spent clearing this land in one year, there would have been little time to raise a crop.[64]

In addition, by asserting that no land was prepared for cultivation between the land booms, North's theory conflicts with other evidence. Some of the land bought from the government was held for resale and clearing at a later date, and the states were also important alternate sources of land. The Southern states in particular were engaged during the 1830's in the popular activity of moving the Indians. The Cherokee, Chickasaw, Creek, and Choctaw Indians had been settled in various parts of Georgia, Alabama, Mississippi, North Carolina, and Tennessee. During the 1830's they were removed to the west of

63. *U. S. Historical Statistics,* p. 239.
64. The estimate of labor needed for clearing land is subject to a wide error, but the estimate would have to be of the wrong order of magnitude to negate the conclusion in the text. Martin Primack, "Land Clearing Under Nineteenth-Century Techniques. Some Preliminary Calculations," *Journal of Economic History,* XXII (December, 1962), 491; Stanley Lebergott, *Manpower in Economic Growth: The American Record since 1800* (New York: McGraw-Hill, 1964), p. 510.

an "Indian Line" (west of the Mississippi River) that was to mark the limit of white settlement. Georgia in particular was active all through this decade in making the Indian land accessible to white settlers, and it would be unreasonable to assume that none of this land was used to grow cotton.[65]

It follows that federal land sales are not a good index of additions to land cleared and ready for cotton. We shall show also that the implications of North's supply curve conflict with conclusions drawn from other, more reliable evidence, and that the curve cannot be accepted for that reason. It will be apparent as the argument continues that it also explains why the hypothesis that the expansion of the money supply caused the price of cotton to rise is similarly defective.

As no mention is made of the movement of demand in either of these hypotheses, we must assume that a subsidiary part of the hypothesis is that the demand for cotton expanded at a constant pace throughout this period. If we do not make this assumption, the hypotheses under discussion are not separate from the hypothesis that increased demand raised the price, and we will have no way to distinguish them. It is possible, of course, that more than one hypothesis is relevant, but North and R. C. O. Matthews both concluded that only supply conditions were relevant, and we are testing this assertion.[66]

A series of demand curves has been drawn in Figure 1, representing, say, possible demand curves for 1831, 1832, 1833, 1834, and 1835. The demand curves show the quantities of cot-

65. Grant Foreman, *Indian Removal: The Emigration of the Five Civilized Tribes of Indians* (Norman, Okla.: University of Oklahoma Press, 1932); Dale Van Every, *Disinherited: The Lost Birthright of the American Indian* (New York: Morrow, 1966); Milton Heath, *Constructive Liberalism: The Role of the State in Economic Development in Georgia to 1860* (Cambridge: Harvard University Press, 1954), pp. 145–46; S. G. McLendon, *History of the Public Domain of Georgia* (Atlanta: Foote & Davies, 1924), pp. 127–29; Mary E. Young, "Indian Removal and Land Allotment: The Civilized Tribes and Jacksonian Justice," *American Historical Review*, LXIV (October, 1958), 31–45.

66. Matthews, pp. 52–54; North, 1961, pp. 71–73.

ton that people were willing to buy in each year at each price. It is generally true that people will buy more goods at a lower price than at a higher price, all other things being equal, and the demand curves consequently slope downward.

These curves are equally spaced, reflecting our assumption that the demand curves shifted outward at a constant rate throughout the 1830's. They intersect the supply curve, S, at the various points shown on the graph. But even though the demand curves are equally spaced, the points of intersection are not. The distance from Q_1 to Q_2 and from Q_2 to Q_3 is larger than the distance from Q_3 to Q_4 and from Q_4 to Q_5. This apparently odd phenomenon is quite easy to explain. As long as the demand curves intersect the supply curve along its elastic portion, they intersect it at approximately the same height. The distance between the points of intersection is consequently almost equal to the distance between the curves. However, when the demand curves intersect the supply curve along its inelastic, upward-sloping portion, they intersect it at progressively higher points. The distance from Q_4 to Q_5 therefore is equal to the distance between D_4 and D_5 minus the distance lost by moving along the demand curve, D_5, from P_4 to P_5. In simpler language, the increase from 1834 to 1835 in the quantity that people would have bought at a given price would have been partially offset by their unwillingness to buy as much at the 1835 price as they would have bought at the 1834 price.

The importance of this offset is related to the slope of the demand curves, or, as economists say, to their elasticity. The steeper the curves—that is, the less the elasticity—the smaller the offset would be. If the curves were vertical, there would be no offset, because it would not matter where on the curve the intersection was. In this case, however, people would buy a given amount of cotton irrespective of the price.

This situation is shown in Figure 2, where the same supply curve as in Figure 1 is intersected by a series of equally spaced vertical demand curves. It can be seen that the intersections of these demand curves with the supply curve are equally spaced.

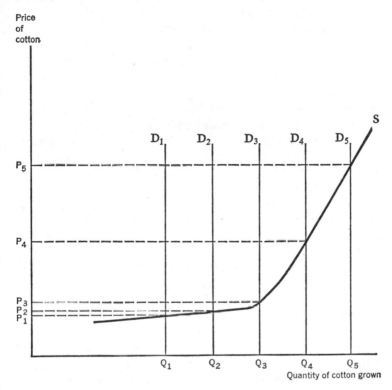

FIGURE 2   Hypothetical Supply and Demand
Curves for Cotton, II

If the quantity of cotton that people were willing to buy in any
one year was independent of the price, a rise in the price would
not have affected the quantities bought.

Turning to the historical record, we find that the quantity of
cotton grown and sold did not grow more slowly in the mid-
1830's than in other years. The quantity of cotton grown rose at

approximately 6 percent a year between 1820 and the Civil War, with remarkably little variation. Part of this variation came in the 1830's, but in this decade the quantity of cotton grown rose faster, not slower, than usual.[67]

The curves in Figure 1 indicate a slower than usual growth during the inflation, and they consequently do not explain the historical events. We must reject them as descriptions of the market at that time. The curves in Figure 2, on the other hand, are roughly consistent with the behavior of prices and quantities during the 1830's; the problem with these curves is that they conflict with other parts of the historical record. In particular, the assumption that the demand for cotton was inelastic—that is, vertical—at this time conflicts with a large body of evidence about the industrial revolution.

The cotton-textile industry was a leading industry in the industrialization both of Britain and of the United States. According to the accounts which can be found in almost any historical work, the increases in the efficiency of cotton-textile production lowered the prices of cotton textiles and increased the quantities demanded. This increase in the quantity demanded then sparked the expansion of the cotton-textile and other industries. The cotton-textile industry expanded because people bought more cotton textiles at their new lower prices than they would have bought at higher prices—that is, because the demand for cotton textiles was not vertical. It did not matter to people whether the price of textiles fell because of increased productivity in their manufacture or because of a lower price of cotton. The price decline was the same, and they acted accordingly. Cotton-textile producers therefore bought more cotton at low prices than they bought at high prices.[68]

67. See the statistical results discussed below.
68. While the elasticity of demand for cotton textiles is not known with precision, recent works show it to have been greater than one in the United States. This means that a rise (fall) in the price of cotton textiles by x percent produced reduced (increased) the quantities demanded by at least x percent also. (Robert B. Zevin, "The Growth of Cotton Textile Production After 1815," forthcoming.) *(Note continues on next page.)*

An inelastic demand curve for cotton therefore is not compatible with an elastic demand curve for cotton textiles. The curves shown in Figure 2 are not consistent with a large body of other data about the industrial revolution, and it is not possible to make North's supply curve consistent with other data on the 1830's.

The preceding arguments militate against acceptance of the third hypothesis presented above as well as the second. Had the price of cotton risen in the absence of a corresponding rise in the demand, then either the quantity sold would have grown less slowly than usual or the demand curve was perfectly inelastic. As we have seen, the former is contrary to fact, while the latter conflicts with what we know of the textile industry and the industrial revolution. Consequently, neither a sudden inelasticity of supply nor the rapid increase in the supply of money in the United States will explain the rise in the price of cotton.

We are left with the first hypothesis: An increase in the demand. But there is no reason to think that this factor operated in isolation. The rejection of the other two hypotheses in isolation implies nothing about their influence in conjunction with a rise in demand. So to see how the various factors interacted, I have described a possible set of supply-and-demand

---

The cotton-textile industry did not vary its output much from year to year in response to business conditions, and part of the variations in the quantity of raw cotton bought reflected variations in inventories. Producers were willing to accumulate inventories at low prices for two reasons. First, if more cotton was available because of an unusually good harvest, producers would buy the cotton to hold until a smaller harvest raised the price. Cotton did not spoil, and credit was available; it was easy to hold cotton stocks for speculative purposes. Second, if more cotton became available on a permanent basis, it would eventually result in an increased production of cotton textiles. Since the quantity of cotton textiles demanded responded to the price, this enlarged quantity of textiles could be sold without an excessive fall in the price. All other things being equal, therefore, a producer who accumulated an inventory at a relatively low price would be able to make it all into textiles over a period of time and sell it at a profit even if every other producer was doing the same. See Paul F. McGouldrick, *New England Textiles in the Nineteenth Century: Profits and Investment* (Cambridge: Harvard University Press, 1968), pp. 9, 29–30, 103–04.

curves for the cotton market and then tested this description to see both how well it explains the historical data and how important various elements were.[69]

The first part of the new hypothesis is that the American price of cotton fluctuated with the British price—that is, that there was a "world price" of cotton. Two factors could have led to a systematic divergence between the American and British prices: The British tariff on raw cotton changed over this period, and increased efficiency in ocean shipping may have decreased the Anglo-American price differential. I therefore attempted to explain the variations in the New Orleans price of cotton by changes in the Liverpool price, the British tariff, and time—the last being a proxy for the effects of increasing efficiency in transportation. The test showed that movements of the British price explain three quarters of the variation of the American price, indicating that we can talk in terms of a single "world price." It also showed that the British tariff on cotton was not important, and that there was no tendency for the British price to fall faster than the American. The British tariff and changes in freight rates may be ignored.

The close connection between the American and British price is not surprising; the United States was the principal supplier of the British industry. The data in Table 3.6 show that the United States supplied over 80 percent of the cotton used in the British industry for most years in the 1830's. They also show that the proportion of the American cotton crop that was used in Britain was not as large as the proportion of British consumption that came from America, and we must consider the demand for cotton from other places. Only about 60 percent of the crop was converted into cloth in Britain, and the remainder was split between American cotton mills and mills in other countries. We know almost nothing about the demand for cot-

69. The discussion for the next few pages is taken from Peter Temin, "The Causes of Cotton-Price Fluctuations in the 1830's," *Review of Economics and Statistics,* XLIX (Nov., 1967), 463–70, where more detail can be found.

TABLE 3.6

Production and Consumption of Cotton, 1830–44

FISCAL YEAR	U. S. PRODUCTION	U. S. EXPORTS	U. K. CONSUMPTION	U. K. CONSUMPTION OF U. S. COTTON	PRICE AT NEW ORLEANS
	(million pounds)				(cents per pound)
1830	365	298	248	202	8.9
1831	350	277	263	197	8.4
1832	385	322	277	202	9.0
1833	390	325	287	221	10.0
1834	445	385	303	269	11.2
1835	460	387	318	284	15.5
1836	508	424	347	290	15.2
1837	540	444	366	321	13.3
1838	683	596	417	431	9.0
1839	522	414	382	312	12.4
1840	790	744	459	449	7.9
1841	644	530	438	320	9.1
1842	668	585	435	369	7.8
1843	973	792	518	535	5.7
1844	837	664	544	470	7.5

SOURCES:
Column 1: U. S. Department of Agriculture, Bureau of Statistics, Circular 32 (1912), "Cotton Crop of the United States, 1790–1911" (Washington, 1912).
Column 2: U. S. Historical Statistics, p. 547.
Column 3: B. R. Mitchell and Phyllis Deane, Abstract of British Historical Statistics (Cambridge, England: Cambridge University Press, 1962), p. 179.
Column 4: Ibid., p. 180.
Column 5: Gray, II, 1027 (redated to be fiscal, rather than crop, years).
NOTE: An alternate series for the production of cotton is given in United States Department of Agriculture, Division of Statistics, *Miscellaneous Series Bulletin 9.* "Production and Price of Cotton for One Hundred Years," by James L. Watkins (Washington, 1895), and quoted in Alfred H. Conrad and John R. Meyer, *The Economics of Slavery* (Chicago: Aldine, 1964), Table 17, p. 76. The author of this series confused crop years (which end in the fall of the year following their designation) and fiscal years (which end in the fall of the year designated). He showed cotton exports for fiscal year 1840, for example, as the exports for crop year 1840, and his data cannot be used for detailed work.

ton in these other countries and therefore cannot hope to discover its year to year variation. We therefore ignore it and
concentrate on the demand from the United States and Britain.

The demand from Britain was by far the largest component
of the demand for cotton, and it is important to see if there were
systematic influences affecting its variation. Two factors come
easily to mind. The argument presented above in refutation of
two of the hypotheses assumed implicitly that prices in Britain
had not risen. If the prices in Britain had risen as much as the
price of cotton, the change would have been in the value of
money, not in the value of cotton relative to other goods, and
there would have been no reason for British purchasers of cotton to restrict their purchases. Only to the extent that the price
of cotton rose faster than other prices is the above argument
valid. The price of cotton did rise faster than other prices—both
in America and in Britain—but we must allow for the rise in
other prices. The first influence affecting the price that British
purchasers could pay for American cotton was therefore the
variation in the overall level of British prices.

The second systematic influence on the price of cotton came
from income variations. We have commented on the temporary
rise in income in the 1830's in the United States, but we have
not yet discussed the parallel movement in England. There was
a boom in both countries, and this boom should have resulted in
a rise in income as well as in prices. The data on British prices
are far better than the data on British income, however, and we
need some indirect indicators of income movements. The wheat
harvest was still probably the most important single influence on
the year-to-year variations in income in Britain. R. C. O.
Matthews, the author of a classic study of the British boom,
chronicled the plentiful harvests of 1832–34 and gave them
credit for helping to initiate the recovery of general prosperity,
and others have followed his lead.[70] We will not be far wrong if

70. Matthews, pp. 30, 206; J. Parry Lewis, *Building Cycles and
Britain's Growth* (New York: St. Martin's Press, 1965), p. 76. Lewis
said, "There is little doubt that the immediate cause of the upswing in

we talk of changes in the British demand for cotton coming from the state of the harvest in place of changes coming from all variations in national income.

In addition to these two systematic influences, there were many other factors affecting the demand in any one year. A large part of British cotton-textile production was exported, and the demand for textiles in the export market would have affected the British demand for cotton. As we do not know much about these demands, we must content ourselves with discussing them on an *ad hoc* basis.

The discussion of demand has isolated four factors affecting the price of cotton: The state of the British wheat harvest, the level of British prices, other non-systematic factors affecting the British demand for cotton, and the American demand for cotton. To these we must add factors coming from the supply side of the market, for the price of cotton—like any price—was set by the interaction of supply and demand. All other things being equal, the larger the cotton crop, the lower the price of cotton would be. We need to discover what influenced the size of the cotton crop.

The supply curve suggested by North showed the supply of cotton to have been a function of the price of cotton and of the amount of land sold by the Federal Government. We have rejected the influence of land sales. We now question whether the quantity of cotton sold in any one year was a function of the price *in that same year*.

Cotton was planted in the year before it was sold, and the weather determined the results of this planting without reference to the price. There are only two ways in which the current price could have affected the quantity sold. Farmers could have reduced the size of the crop by not harvesting it, and farmers

---

1833 was the good harvest." This view has been confirmed by the national income estimates presented by Phyllis Deane, "New Estimates of Gross National Product for the United Kingdom, 1830–1914," *Review of Income and Wealth,* XIV (June, 1968), 95–112. These new estimates unfortunately appeared too late to be used in the present study.

could have held stocks of cotton which they ran down when prices were high and built up when prices were low. There is no indication that not harvesting the crop was a widespread practice. Many of the expenses of raising cotton, such as the maintenance of slaves, were fixed costs, and many others preceded knowledge of the price at which cotton could be sold. As these expenses were sunk costs, the price of cotton had only to exceed the extra cost of harvesting to bring it onto the market. There is also no evidence that farmers held stocks of cotton. There were stocks of variable size in the United States and England, but these stocks had passed through the market and been counted as part of the crop. The accumulation of stocks was a market transaction, and it therefore appears as an increase in the demand rather than a reduction of the supply. As a result, the amount of cotton sold in any one year was independent of the price in that year.[71]

This argument does not exclude the price of the previous year or years as an influence on the supply of cotton, and it is reasonable to expect that the amount of cotton planted was dependent on the price in the year in which the planting was done—that is, the year before the cotton was sold. When estimated by statistical means, this influence turns out to be very small. The price of cotton was quite variable, and plantation owners did not assume that the price would remain constant from one year to the next. Implicit in most accounts of the 1830's is the assumption that cotton growers projected the high prices of 1835 and 1836 into the future, but if they did, this was the result of the boom psychology of the 1830's, not of a general frame of mind.[72]

71. American stocks, if we can believe the data, stayed near 40,000 bales from 1833 to 1837. A bale weighed 350–75 pounds. See Note to Table 3.6.
72. Plantation owners may have predicted prices a year in advance by the use of some kind of weighted average of past prices. This would be a more sophisticated method than projecting the current price ahead one year, and it would take account of more data. It is hard to test the influence of this kind of behavior, however, because the growth of cotton production was exceedingly regular. This may have been because cotton growers looked at the fluctuating price and assumed that the price would

Since we have rejected the use of federal land sales as an index of changes in cotton-growing capacity, a new measure of capacity is needed. The use of land as a measure of capacity assumed that the output per acre of cotton was reasonably constant. It is equally reasonable to assume that the output of cotton per man varied little from year to year. Then if land had been rather freely available from one source or another, the supply of labor—rather than the supply of land—would have been the restraining factor in cotton production.

The average price of land sold by the Federal Government stayed quite constant near the official minimum price of $1.25 per acre. It did not rise above this figure in the boom years of 1835 and 1836, indicating that large amounts of land could be purchased at a roughly constant cost.[73] The supply of land available to grow cotton in any year was a function of the land cleared in previous years, but the land cleared in previous years was not a function of the availability of land. Land was always available; the rate at which it was cleared and brought into production depended on the growth of the agricultural labor force.

We do not have estimates of the annual growth rate of this labor force, but we may assume that it grew with the population. The size of the population also is not known in every year, but we may employ the common assumption that it grew at an even rate between census years. As the rate of growth of population did not vary much from decade to decade in the antebellum period, we assume simply that the growth of cotton-growing capacity grew at an even rate over time. With this assumption, we can explain 96 percent of the annual variation in the size of the cotton crop from 1820 to 1860.[74]

be near an average of the prices in all years, because they had rather fixed ideas about the prices at which they would sell their crop, or because their plans were so insensitive to their expectations about year-to-year price variations that they did not bother to formulate a set of expectations. All of these patterns would have produced the same actions, and we cannot discriminate among them.

73. *U. S. Historical Statistics*, pp. 239, 712.

74. More technically, a regression of the logarithm of the cotton crop on time explains 96 percent of its variance.

It must not be supposed that the weather has been forgotten in this derivation. The cotton crop did not grow at an absolutely even rate through time, and the minor part of its variance not explained by our hypothesis should be attributed to the weather. The weather in any one year was not closely related to the weather in adjoining years—that is, a good harvest in one year did not increase the probability of a good one the next year, and this attribution is valid only if the unexplained part of the cotton crop's variation showed a similar pattern. The deviations of the actual cotton crop from the crop expected by a projection of steady growth were not correlated with each other, and the inference that they were caused by variations in the weather can be accepted.

We have now listed five factors that could have caused the price of cotton to change in any one year: The four components of demand listed earlier and the variation in the harvest. The calculation of the relative importance of the five factors is complex and has been described elsewhere. We can say here only that the assumptions and inferences of the past few pages have been subjected to a statistical test which both demonstrated their appropriateness and quantified their importance.[75]

The general picture of the cotton market shown in Figures 1 and 2 is replaced by the one shown in Figure 3. The supply of cotton in any one year was not related to the price in that year, and it shifted outward each year by an amount determined both by the effects of the long-term trend and the harvest of that year. The quantity of cotton demanded in any one year depended on the price of cotton, and the demand curves conse-

---

75. As we are interested in a particular rise in the price of cotton, we restrict our attention to changes in these factors that caused the price to deviate from its long-term trend. The price of cotton was falling slowly in the antebellum years, and we try to explain the upward deviation from this trend in the 1830's. To do so, we observe the deviation of the various factors influencing the price from their trends and assess their impact on the price of cotton. For instance, the long-term growth of the cotton crop is not important in explaining the deviation of the price from its trend; only the short-term variation coming from the annual fluctuations of the harvest is important.

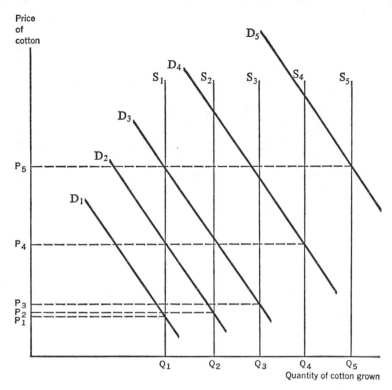

FIGURE 3 Estimated Supply and Demand
Curves for Cotton

quently are not vertical. (We argued above that this had to be;
the statistical test showed that our description of the market was
consistent with it.) The demand curve was also rising in the
1830's, but it rose more rapidly after 1834 than it had before.
This is illustrated by the larger shift between D_3 and D_4 than
between the earlier demand curves. The result was that the price
was higher in the fourth and fifth periods shown than in the
earlier periods. It should be noted that the points of intersection
of the successive demand and supply curves are the same as in

Figure 2; Figures 2 and 3 represent two explanations of the same data.

But this graph cannot tell us why the demand rose rapidly, nor is it precise enough to show the different rates of change of supply in different years. A more precise view of the factors causing the price of cotton to rise in the 1830's is shown in Table 3.7.

The deviations of the cotton price from its trend are shown in the first column, where the ratio of the actual to the trend price is shown. A figure of less than 1 indicates that the actual price was below the trend; a figure larger than 1, that it was above the trend. The influence of the various factors is shown in the remaining columns, also as deviations from trend, and the ratio in the first column is the product of the ratios in all the other columns. A figure less than 1 indicates that a factor was depressing the price below its long-term trend; a figure larger than 1, that it was increasing the price.

The influence of the supply of cotton is shown in the second column of Table 3.7. It acted to decrease the price of cotton below its long-term trend throughout the inflationary years. Not only was there no restriction or inelasticity of supply, but the cotton harvest was better than usual. Had there been no increase in demand, the influence of supply alone would have acted to keep the price of cotton low.

Offsetting this supply influence were expansionary influences coming from three factors affecting the demand. The British wheat harvest was good in 1832, 1833, and 1834; it was less good in 1835, and only average in 1836 and 1837.[76] The influence of the good harvest began to make itself felt in 1833 and continued through 1837, when the stocks accumulated in the good harvests had been exhausted. The availability of cheap bread freed income to be spent on cotton goods, and the demand for cotton rose.

76. Matthews, p. 30; quoting Thomas Tooke, *A History of Prices and of the State of the Circulation, from 1793 to 1856*. Six vols. (London, 1838–57).

Of equal importance was the rise in the American demand which brought it from a below-average position in 1833 to an average level in 1835 and 1836. We do not know why the demand was so low at the start of the inflation, but it seems

TABLE 3.7

Factorization of the Ratio of the Cotton Price to its Trend by Cause, 1833–41

Factors due to:

FISCAL YEAR	TOTAL RATIO	SUPPLY OF COTTON	BRITISH HARVEST	OTHER BRITISH DEMAND	BRITISH PRICE LEVEL	AMERICAN DEMAND
1833	.93	1.01	1.01	1.26	.92	.78
1834	1.05	.96	1.11	1.17	.97	.86
1835	1.47	.98	1.26	1.22	.97	1.00
1836	1.46	.95	1.21	1.16	1.07	1.02
1837	1.29	.95	1.09	.95	1.03	1.26
1838	.88	.85	.94	1.26	1.04	.86
1839	1.23	1.06	1.02	.95	1.14	1.04
1840	.79	.82	1.00	.97	1.13	.88
1841	.93	1.00	1.05	.86	1.07	.97

SOURCE: *Temin, 1967.*

clear that it rose because of the general price rise. The demand for cotton from the American textile industry would not in itself have raised the price as high as it went, but the demand for textiles was high and profits were too.[77]

Finally, the rise in the British price level exerted a smaller inflationary force on the price of cotton. As all prices rose in Britain, British buyers could pay more for cotton without discomfort. (The demand for cotton in Britain unrelated to the wheat harvest—that is, the domestic demand unaffected by the harvest plus the export demand—was high during these years, but it did not rise. It helped to sustain the high price of cotton, but it did not encourage it to rise.)

The price of cotton rose, therefore, for a variety of reasons,

77. McGouldrick, p. 81.

some British, some American. It rose more than the average of all American prices, and this extra rise may be attributed to the rise in British demand. Had demand risen in America alone, the price of cotton would have risen less than half as much as it did, which would have brought its rise closer to the average.[78] As we turn to the inflationary effects of the price rise, this fact will be of some importance.

As we said at the beginning of this discussion, the rise in the price of cotton both helped and hindered the inflation. On the negative side, it encouraged the land boom. On the positive side, the rise in the British demand for cotton increased the inflation. It increased the amount of cotton which British buyers were willing to buy at any given price. Since cotton was a major export to England, this reduced the trade deficit at any price. The price rise also encouraged British investors to export capital to the American South in the same way as it encouraged Americans to buy land. This increased the trade deficit that the Americans could sustain at any given price without losing specie to Britain. Since specie was the basis of the inflation, both effects aided the price rise.

It is hard to quantify the offsetting effects of the rise in cotton prices, and we do not know if the net effect was positive or negative. This price—like any other price—was affected by the particular supply-and-demand conditions in its own market. It certainly did not cause the rise in the general price level; the reasons for the inflation have been set forth in great detail, and they do not include the changes in the market for cotton. The same statement cannot be made about the causes for the deflation that followed this inflation, but that is a story for the next chapter.

78. It is hard to say how close it would have brought the change in the cotton price to the change in the average price, since the former is a part of the latter. Had the price of cotton risen less, the overall price index would have risen less, and it is hard to know exactly how close the two new indexes would have been.

4

The Panic of 1837

ON THE FOURTH OF MARCH, 1837, Martin Van Buren succeeded Andrew Jackson as President of the United States. The inflation was at its height, but all was not well. Workers in New York had rioted in February to protest the high price of food, there was "pressure" in the money markets, and interest rates on short-term loans (the discount rate) stood at 2 percent a month, or 24 percent a year. The crisis continued after Van Buren took office, and accounts of failures in New Orleans and elsewhere continued to reach New York in April with unabated frequency.[1] By the beginning of the following month, the crisis had become a panic. The pressure was too great for the banks to bear, and they "suspended payment"—that is, they refused to pay specie for their outstanding notes and deposits at par. The banks in New York City suspended payment on May 10, but the suspension soon became national. Banks in Albany, Hartford, New Hampshire, Philadelphia, Providence, and Baltimore suspended on May 11; banks in Mobile and Boston, on May 12; banks in New Orleans, on May 13; and so on. It was asserted by contemporaries that the banks in New York and New Orleans acted independently, and the difference in the dates of suspension—which was not long enough for word to travel from New York and New Orleans—supports this view.[2]

1. *Niles' Weekly Register* (Baltimore, 1811–49), LI (February 18, 1837), 400; (February 25, 1837), 403–04; LII (March 18, 1837), 33; LII (April 8, 1837), 82.
2. *Ibid.,* LII (June 3, 1837), 210.

Effects of the Crisis

"The suspension of specie payments . . . is in fact a state of general bankruptcy." [3] This comment by a contemporary observer needs to be interpreted in a very narrow sense. Bank notes and bank deposits were issued with a promise to redeem them in specie at their face value; in a moral sense, a failure to fulfill this obligation was perhaps bankruptcy. It was also illegal in many states, although the laws on this matter were seldom enforced.[4] But the banks were not bankrupt. They did not close their doors. They did not go out of business. They simply refused to pay the full face value for their notes and deposits, and the actions that might have led from that decision to a court declaration of insolvency were not undertaken.

The suspension of payments in the 19th century was not at all like the bank suspension of 1933. In the 20th century the banks were completely closed for a week, and many of them were declared bankrupt in the course of that week. In the 19th century the banks refused to fulfill only one of their obligations, and they continued to fulfill others. In fact, since they were no longer obligated to maintain the price of their notes and deposits in terms of gold and silver, they were able to issue them more easily than before.[5]

Let us examine this process in more detail. Banks held only fractional reserves, based on the assumption that only a small percentage of their outstanding obligations would have to be redeemed in any short period of time. When faced by a sudden demand for specie—whether from panic or any other cause—the banks tried to obtain more specie by calling in loans. The loans were repaid either in notes and checks or in specie, and the notes and checks of other banks received in this process

3. Appleton, p. 48, quoting a letter he wrote to the *Boston Daily Advertiser,* November 15, 1837.
4. Gallatin, p. 36.
5. Hammond, p. 478; Friedman and Schwartz, pp. 167, 328–29.

were presented to the other banks for payment in specie. Each bank thereby attempted to transfer the demand for specie from it to other banks, and the demand for specie spread throughout the banking system. As the pressure spread, people feared that banks might suspend payments, and no one returned loans in the form of specie. The banks then pressed each other for specie that none of them could obtain. With fractional reserves, there just was not enough specie in banks to cover all the outstanding notes and deposits.

The results of this process, of course, were disastrous. With banks calling in loans—or refusing to renew expiring loans—merchants were not able to get the credit they were used to. They therefore were not able to fulfill their obligations. If the panic continued for any length of time, the merchants would fail; they would be truly bankrupt.

But there was an alternative to this sequence. As merchants began to fail, the banks refused to pay specie for notes at a fixed price. This established a free market for notes in terms of specie. The banks then did not need to get specie from other banks or from an unwilling public, and they did not have to call in loans and impose great hardship on their debtors. If people wanted specie for notes or deposits, the specie-price (the price in specie) of notes and deposits would fall until people no longer wanted to change. Suspension as practiced in the 19th century was not bankruptcy; one might say it was an alternative to bankruptcy.

In addition to the effect just noted, the suspension of payments also put an end to fears that the banks would suspend payments. As long as there was the possibility that the price of notes and deposits would fall relative to that of specie, there was an incentive to exchange them for specie. Once the price was freed, it fell to the point where there was no incentive to make this trade—that is, to the point where the people who thought the specie-price of notes and deposits would fall further (and who therefore wished to sell them) were offset by those who thought their specie-price would rise (and who therefore wanted to buy them). The discount on notes and deposits relative to specie stabilized, and the panic—the anticipation of worse things to come—ended.

The banks were no longer under pressure, and because they were under no obligation to maintain the price of their notes and deposits relative to specie, they could allow the public to have more of them. (If there were "too many" outstanding, their price would fall, but the banks would not lose their specie and become insolvent.) Monetary "pressure" was transformed into monetary ease. The discount rate on commercial paper in Boston and New York, which provides a good index of monetary "pressure," fell. We stated before that this rate was about 2 percent a month in early 1837. It had been at that level since the fall of 1836, and it fluctuated around that level through May of 1837. After the suspension of payments in that month, the discount rate fell sharply, going from 18 percent a year (1.5 percent a month) at the start of June to 6 percent a year (one half percent a month) at the end. This was the cost of borrowing money in previous periods of relative calm, such as 1831–33, and it was maintained for several months thereafter.[6]

Suspension thus solved one class of problems—namely, those arising from the inability to borrow money in a panic—but it created others. Debtors were legally obligated to pay debts in legal tender, that is, in specie. Before suspension, creditors were willing to take bank notes or checks because they could be exchanged for specie at very little cost. When banks suspended payments, the cost of getting specie for notes or checks rose dramatically, and bank obligations were no longer a good substitute for specie. Most people, however, were both debtor and creditor. They did not want to pay off their debts in coin, and they consequently did not insist that people pay debts owed to them in coin. Within any single locality, therefore, business continued on the basis of bank notes and checks, and specie was not used as money.[7]

6. Smith and Cole, p. 192.
7. Gallatin, p. 23.

Freed of the necessity to pay specie for notes and deposits, banks were also freed of the necessity to hold reserves. As we said, this made it easier for them to issue new loans. In fact, it made it too easy, and some way was needed to limit the activities of banks. Banks in some cities accordingly substituted some kind of communal action for the requirement to redeem notes in specie. In Boston, the banks resolved to act together during the suspension, to regulate each other's expansion by inspecting each other's books and refusing to accept the notes or checks of any bank if too many had been issued by that bank.[8] It is indeed ironic that this action, taken during the demoralization of the banking system, should represent the closest approach to modern banking practice seen in the antebellum period.

Debts owed to persons outside the immediate locality were a different matter. Debts owed between localities often did not offset each other exactly, and banks normally financed temporary regional deficits. But banks in New York were unhappy to receive an obligation of a bank in Charleston when it was not redeemable in specie. If the obligations were to finance a deficit, the New Yorkers did not owe money to the bank in Charleston, and they were not close enough to know of action by the Charleston bank that would preserve the value of its obligations. Like the local merchant, they would not refuse to take notes or checks because this would destroy their business. But they would be less happy at doing so, and they would express this emotion by charging more for their services—that is, by accepting the bank notes or deposits at less than par.[9]

This process was at its strongest in international transactions. Merchants owing debts to England were expected to pay in pounds. The price of pounds was fixed in gold, and the premium on pounds moved with the premium on gold. The debts of British merchants were typically to other Englishmen, and these creditors expected to receive full face value for their

8. *Niles' Weekly Register,* LII (May 27, 1837), pp. 195–96. The banks also agreed to accept specie for special specie deposits.
9. Bills drawn on New Orleans fell to a discount of 8 to 10 percent in New York in May, 1838. Elliot, 1845, p. 1170.

loans. The merchants therefore wanted full value from the Americans, and the Americans were obligated to purchase specie or foreign exchange at a premium to remit to England. The dealers in foreign trade suffered the most from devaluation.

The extent of this suffering can be inferred from the data in Table 4.1. The price of bills on London rose with the premium

TABLE 4.1

Premium on Specie at New York, 1837–38

DATE	GOLD	SILVER
	(percent)	
May 24, 1837	5–10	
July 1, 1837	10–12	10.5–11
October 4, 1837	5–5.5	5.5–5.75
December 2, 1837	4.5–5	4.5–5
January 3, 1838	2.5–3	2.5–3
February 28, 1838	2.5–3	2.5–3

SOURCE: *Elliot, 1845, pp. 1146–47. The rates were for "new coinage" of gold (post-1834 coinage) and silver half-dollars.*

on gold, and the exchange rate explicit in the bill prices rose to a premium of about 10 percent in the second and third quarters of 1837.[10] The suffering caused by the suspension therefore was real, but it was also limited. The maximum devaluation of the dollar was only about 10 percent.

Prices in the United States fell by one quarter from their peak in February, 1837, to their trough in September. This price fall, which continued for some months after the exchange rate began to rise, made imports even more expensive relative to domestic goods than the data in Table 4.1 imply, and it is not surprising that imports in fiscal 1838 were less than three quarters of the imports the previous year.[11]

10. Smith and Cole, p. 190; Davis and Hughes, Table A-2, p. 72. The premium on specie in Cincinnati was similar to the New York premium. Thomas Senior Berry, *Western Prices Before 1861* (Cambridge: Harvard University Press, 1943), pp. 590–91.

11. Table 3.2; North, 1960, p. 605.

When the demand for a commodity falls, its price usually falls, and it has been common to see the fall in the overall price level in 1837 as the result of a general fall in the demand for commodities. The rise in demand that produced the inflation before 1837 was produced by a rise in the supply of money. Could the fall in prices in 1837 have been caused by a fall in demand deriving from a decline in this supply?

The supply of money fell by about 15 percent from late 1836 to late 1837, roughly the same amount that prices fell at the same time. Prices had been somewhat lower in the fall of 1837 than they were by year's end, but we do not have data on the money supply for the intermediate period. Consequently, the available data support the simple hypothesis that prices fell because the supply of money fell, although they are not sufficiently complete to rule out alternative, more complex causal chains.[12]

The supply of money fell in 1837 despite a specie inflow. The increased amount of specie available was offset both by the banking contraction and a decline in the willingness of the public to hold bank obligations. After an initial expansion following the panic, banks increased their reserve ratios in order to be in a strong position when they resumed specie payments. They could not know how hard it would be to preserve the parity between bank notes and deposits and specie; the more specie they had relative to their notes and deposits, the better able to support this parity they would be. The public—which included the Federal Government in these data—had learned that bank obligations were not always "as good as gold," and that they could lose 10 percent of their value in a few months. They refused to hold bank notes and deposits, and the sharp rise in the proportion of money held by the public in coin was the principal cause of the decline in the supply of money.[13]

Having less money, people demanded fewer goods. This appears to have been the primary cause of the price decline. We

12. Tables 3.2, 3.3.
13. See the discussion of Table 3.3 for the relation of these magnitudes to the supply of money.

may well ask if the fall in demand caused production to fall as well. Evidence of economic distress from 1837 is not hard to find. It is of two kinds. The first recounts the failures of business firms, and the second chronicles unemployment. Businesses can fail because the price declines, and a failed business can reopen under a new name and unencumbered by past debts in a matter of days. Failures therefore do not necessarily indicate a decline in demand or in production. Unemployment, on the other hand, is an unequivocal sign of a decline in production. Fifty thousand workers were reported idle in New York sometime in 1837, 2,000 unemployed were reported in Lynn (Massachusetts), and cotton mills in Boston and Lowell were idle. One report even claimed that nine tenths of the factories in the East had ceased production. Discounting the last observation, most of the evidence of unemployment concerns a few major urban centers. As only about 10 percent of the population lived in large cities, unemployment would have had to be very large in the cities to represent a major cost to society.[14] Agricultural production does not seem to have been affected by the crisis, and other records of production not dependent on prices show a continued rise to 1839. The deflation of 1837 was mild and short-lived; it does not seem to have caused major distress in the economy.[15]

The Specie Circular

Explanations for a condition of general distress are never lacking. Not only explanations, but often villains are sought,

14. *U. S. Historical Statistics,* p. 9. The data refer to cities with populations of 2,500 or more.

15. See Samuel Rezneck, "Social History of an American Depression, 1837–1843," *American Historical Review,* XL (July, 1935), 662–87; and Lebergott, pp. 176–77, for records of unemployment. They both cumulate evidence on unemployment, business failures, and price declines; this clearly is invalid. Smith and Cole's index of the volume of trade, p. 73, showed a fall in 1837, but it was compiled partly from series that depended on price changes and is not a good index of the *volume* of trade alone. See the discussion of these and other data in Chapter 5, below.

and Andrew Jackson has usually been cast in this role. The Deposit Act, passed by Congress in June, 1836, and the Specie Circular issued a month later are the policies that have qualified him for that role, and we must examine the effects of these policies to see if it suits him. The Specie Circular was the more important policy to contemporaries, and we begin our discussion with it.

The Specie Circular was an executive order issued in July, 1836, as an antidote to the inflationary effects of the distribution of the surplus. It said that after August 15, only specie and Virginia land scrip would be accepted in payment for public land, with the exception that up to December 15 bank obligations could be used as payment for purchases of less than 320 acres by actual settlers.[16]

The Specie Circular is supposed to have had two effects: It is said to have drained specie from the East to be used in Western land purchases and also to have decreased the volume of these purchases. To the extent that the Circular had the latter effect, it could not have had the former, and vice versa. These effects are alternatives, not a combination. We examine them in turn.

The movement of specie is exceedingly problematical. There are contemporary observations of specie movements that we have no reason to distrust.[17] Yet the banking statistics that have survived show no evidence of a drain of specie from Eastern banks.

If specie had moved from Eastern to Western banks in late 1836, reserve ratios in the West should have risen relative to those in the East in 1836, but the data in Table 3.4 show little

16. Bourne, p. 27; *Niles' Weekly Register,* L (July 16, 1836), 337. There is considerable doubt in the literature as to the date on which the circular took effect, some historians citing August 15 and others, December 15. To choose a date, we need to know the proportion of sales that were made to actual settlers in lots smaller than 320 acres. As these data have not been compiled, the point is moot.

17. Gallatin, p. 31; Bourne, p. 35; McGrane, pp. 62–63; Matthews, p. 55. Swisher, pp. 331–32, said the Specie Circular *helped* the deposit banks by bringing them specie. If so, it acted to forestall a panic!

evidence of such a shift. The Northwest was the only Western region to show a rising reserve ratio in 1836, and this rise was not large. Even had it been large, it would not necessarily have indicated a drain of specie from the East. The total amount of specie in the system was increasing, and the West could have accumulated more specie without drawing it from the East. The data in Table 4.2 show this to have been the case. Specie re-

TABLE 4.2

Distribution of Specie in State Banks by Region, 1834–37
(millions of dollars)

END OF YEAR	NEW ENGLAND	MIDDLE ATLANTIC	SOUTH-EAST	SOUTH-WEST	NORTH-WEST	TOTAL
Treasury Data						
1834	1.8	12.0	2.9	1.6	2.6	20.9
1835	2.4	12.1	7.0	6.0	4.6	32.1
1836	2.6	11.7	7.1	7.9	5.7	35.0
1837	2.9	10.0	6.1	6.6	5.7	31.3
Van Fenstermaker's Data						
1834	2.9	11.9	3.5	3.4	2.5	24.3
1835	3.6	12.2	5.1	5.5	4.5	31.0
1836	3.6	15.2	7.6	7.7	5.7	39.8
1837	4.3	13.4	6.0	6.9	5.9	36.4

SOURCES: *See Appendix and Notes to Table 3.4.*

serves of banks increased in the Northwest, but they also increased in most other regions. The only decline shown in 1836 is a 3 percent decline in the specie reserves in the Middle Atlantic States, a decline that is only shown in one of the two sources.

The movement of specie to the West induced by the Specie Circular in 1836 therefore was not large enough to have had even a minor role in causing the suspension of payments in May, 1837. In other words, either the purchases made in late 1836 were purchases of less than 320 acres by actual settlers, or the same gold and silver coins were being used more than once for land sales. The same coins could have been used because banks were willing to exchange their obligations for specie at par throughout 1836. When the government received specie for land, it deposited it in a local bank, making it available for another purchase. If the same coins were used more than once, the amount of specie needed for land purchases would be less than the amount of land sales themselves.[18]

During 1837, the total amount of specie used for banking reserves fell, but the West as well as the East lost specie. The government was not depositing its revenues in banks in late 1837, and if specie had traveled west to be used to buy land, it would have landed in the Treasury's hands. The Treasury, however, did not increase its holdings of specie during 1837, and specie could only have traveled west in 1837 if it was held by individuals at the end of the year—that is, if it was not used to purchase land.[19] There is thus no evidence that the Specie Circular pulled specie to the West in either 1836 or 1837.

The Specie Circular, therefore, did not bring on the suspension of payments by denuding Eastern banks of specie. Why then was it so important—as it clearly was—to contemporaries?

18. This sounds a little like the way in which the reserve ratios were supposed to have been drawn down in the inflation, a mechanism that was said in Chapter 3 not to have worked. The difference is that the reserve ratio would not have to fall when specie was used over again: The deposits of individuals would decline as the government's deposits rose. If they did not, then the process would be the one described in Chapter 3, and the reserve ratios should have fallen.

Richard H. Timberlake, Jr., "The Specie Circular and Sales of Public Lands: A Comment," *Journal of Economic History*, XXV (September, 1965), 414–16, noted also that the velocity of money—that is, the number of times a given dollar was used in an income-generating transaction—was about five, and that specie would then be used five times in one year for land purchases. The problem with this is that land purchases are not income-generating transactions, and the income velocity of money is not a relevant datum.

19. The *Report* of the U. S. Comptroller of the Currency, 1896, I, 544, estimated Treasury specie as $5 million at both the start and end of 1837. An alternate series shows that the balance in Treasury offices (as opposed to depository banks) rose only from $0.7 million to $1 million. Taus, p. 268.

They may have been mistaken in their views of its effects, or they may have thought that its effect on the volume of land sales was more important than its effect on bank reserves. The quarterly volume of land sales is shown in Table 4.3 for the years surrounding the boom. The spectacular rise in sales in 1835 and 1836 that has been discussed above is evident. The peak sales

TABLE 4.3

Land Sales by the Federal Government, Quarterly, 1833–40 (millions of dollars)

	I	II	III	IV	TOTAL
1833	.6	.8	.8	2.0	4.2
1834	1.1	1.0	1.0	3.1	6.1
1835	2.0	3.1	4.1	6.9	16.2
1836	5.8	8.4	5.9	4.8	24.9
1837	3.5	1.8	.7	.9	6.9
1838	.5	.5	.7	2.2	4.0
1839	1.8	1.7	1.3	1.7	6.5
1840	1.0	.8	.5	.5	2.7

SOURCE: *Smith and Cole, p. 185. These data differ slightly from those in Timberlake, 1965, which were partially interpolated from annual tables, and from those in U. S. Historical Statistics, p. 712, which are presented on an annual basis only.*

occurred in the second quarter of 1836—that is, the quarter just preceding the issuance of the Specie Circular—and they fell thereafter. It seems obvious that the Specie Circular arrested the boom.

But how would the Specie Circular have affected land sales? On the supply side, it made public land more expensive. As long as banks exchanged specie for notes and deposits at par, this extra cost was small; when the banks suspended payment, it became a serious added cost. But people were buying land in the expectation of future gain, expectations that were sanguine to the point of folly. The data in Table 4.1 indicate that the extra cost resulting from the necessity to use specie instead of bank obligations was only on the order of 10 percent. It is hard to see that this relatively small increase in the price would have reduced the quantity bought by as much as it fell in 1836 and 1837.

If the effects on the supply side were small, the effects on the demand side must have been large if the Specie Circular had any effect. The circular must have sharply decreased the demand for public land. But to the extent that the circular reduced the supply of land available to future purchasers, it could well have increased the current demand for speculative purchases.[20] The net effect of the circular on land sales depended on its effects on people's expectations. The circular was issued at a time of great public excitement over the public revenues, shortly after the passage of a very important bill distributing the Treasury surplus to the states. It was an attempt to offset the distribution bill and to avoid supporting the speculative boom in progress.[21] The government certainly had the power to end the boom—if not by this means, then by others—and the realization that it might use this power should have sobered potential purchasers of land. The Specie Circular therefore decreased the demand for land, not by its direct effect on the market for land, but by its effect on expectations about the economy as a whole. People suspected that the boom was going to end, and they refrained from buying land.

Paradoxically, however, the diminution of land sales may have added to the inflation. Purchases of land are usually seen in the secondary literature as a part of national income.[22] Nevertheless, the sale of land does not indicate the production of goods or services. No additional goods entered the economy through the purchase of land; existing resources simply changed hands. (The purchase may have led to cultivation and therefore

20. Bourne, p. 28.
21. Benton, I, 676–78.
22. Meerman; Richard H. Timberlake, Jr., "The Specie Circular and the Distribution of the Surplus," *Journal of Political Economy*, LXVIII (April, 1960), 109–17.

to more goods, but it is the cultivation of land that produces income.) The fall in land sales therefore did not indicate a diminution of income and an end to the expansion. To the extent that it freed money for other uses, it indicated the exact opposite. Money that had been used for land sales could be used for other purchases. These purchases could be income-generating, and they would probably be for goods in less elastic supply than land. We showed in Chapter 3 that the sale of land acted as a "sink" for the extra money supply of the mid-1830's because unlimited quantities could be bought without raising the price. If these funds were directed elsewhere, they would cause prices to rise and the inflation to continue.[23]

The effect of the Specie Circular on the inflation was thus the sum of two offsetting effects. On the one hand, the circular caused people to re-examine their sanguine expectations of ever-increasing prices and profits. On the other, it made one of the goods in demand harder to buy, diverting demand to other goods. The first effect acted to reduce the demand for goods and therefore to arrest the inflation. The second acted to increase the demand for goods other than land and therefore—by diverting demand from a commodity with a fixed price to commodities in less elastic supply—to accelerate the inflation. Prices continued to rise in late 1836 while land sales fell, suggesting that the second effect was stronger than the first.[24]

Similarly, the effect of the Specie Circular on production is uncertain. The diversion of demand from land sales to other markets should have led to an increase in production. Land was not produced by the economy, but the other goods demanded in its stead might easily have been. On the other hand, if the total demand fell, the demand for goods other than land may have fallen also. Since prices continued to rise after the promulgation of the circular, it is unlikely that the latter effect was large.

Even though the economic impact of the Specie Circular

23. Timberlake, *ibid.*, noted this effect of a decrease in land sales.
24. Table 3.2.

was small, it was still an important indicator of the government's attitude. Contemporary attention to the circular must be understood in this connection.[25] Shortly before the banks suspended payment, the *New York Courier and Enquirer* said: "The aspect of affairs is decidedly brighter in Wall Street today, and if the executive would now repeal the specie circular, all would be well." [26] This typical plea cannot be interpreted as an assertion of the close day-to-day connection of the New York financial market and the market for Western land. It refers instead to the dependence of the financial market on expectations about the future course of the economy and the dependence of these expectations in turn on the government's policy. The Specie Circular itself could not have had a great effect on the economy, but it functioned as a signal of the Administration's intentions.

This discussion of the Specie Circular follows our analysis of the preceding inflation. Our description of the inflation differs sharply from the traditional account, and it is not surprising that our evaluation of the impact of the Specie Circular does likewise. Contemporaries thought that the inflation had been caused by an expansion of the money supply without a corresponding increase of specie reserves. The Specie Circular was a measure designed to inhibit or even reverse this process, and it seemed like a stronger measure to contemporaries than it appears here.

It should also be noted that the Specie Circular was not the only measure affecting expectations in early 1837. In particular, the Treasury was distributing its surplus to the states, and the price of cotton was falling. Both of these events had important

25. To the extent that the Specie Circular operated through expectations, it operated from the date of its announcement, not from its effective date. As soon as the measure was known, expectations changed, and the demand for land changed with them. This phenomenon therefore may explain the timing of the peak in land sales shown in Table 4.3.

26. *Niles' Weekly Register*, LII (April 29, 1837), 129.

repercussions which led people to question the continuance of the boom. The effects of the Specie Circular on expectations cannot be separated from the effects of these other events.

The Distribution of the Surplus

The distribution of the Federal Government's surplus that took place in 1837 was also in the forefront of contemporary discussion, although it was not accorded as prominent a place as the Specie Circular. If the latter was less important than contemporaries thought, however, recent thought indicates that the former may well have been more. In fact, one author has asserted recently that "the relatively small amount of specie actually withdrawn from the deposit banks [for the distribution] provided the jeweled pivot for a major bank-credit contraction." [27] Let us examine this modern view of the crisis in detail.

The act authorizing the distribution of the surplus was passed in June, 1836. It dealt with two main topics, the distribution of the government's surplus, and the regulation of deposit banks. On the first, the bill provided for the deposit with the states of the balance in the federal Treasury in excess of $5 million on January 1, 1837. This was to be an interest-free loan to the states, but as it has never been recalled, it is usually spoken of as a distribution rather than a deposit. The distribution was to take place in four equal installments at three-month intervals, starting January 1, 1837. On the second topic, the bill imposed several regulations on the deposit banks, the most important of which was that a deposit bank could not hold government deposits in an amount in excess of three quarters of its paid-in capital.[28]

27. Timberlake, 1960, p. 112.
28. *Niles' Weekly Register,* L (June 25, 1836), 290–91; U. S. Treasury, *Report on Finances,* December, 1836, p. 13; Harry N. Scheiber, "The Pet Banks in Jacksonian Politics and Finance, 1833–41," *Journal of Economic History,* XXIII (June, 1963), 196–214. The act was Jackson's substitute for Clay's similar proposal. Raynor G. Wellington, *The Political and Sectional Influence of the Public Lands, 1828–42* (Cambridge: Riverside Press, 1914), Chapter 3.

The first measure—the actual distribution—has received far more attention from historians than the second. As with the Specie Circular, we have many stories of specie movements caused by the distribution. Unlike the earlier accounts, however, no unified direction to the movements was noted here.[29] If the specie was moving back and forth, there is no way our statistics could show whether or not it existed. If the specie moving to the West (perhaps moving partly because of the Specie Circular) was balanced by specie moving to the East, the data shown in Table 4.2 could only show this movement by a decline in the total amount of specie used for bank reserves. As it is likely that banks counted specie in transit as part of their reserves when they reported their condition, even this cannot be counted upon to appear. Consequently, the movement of specie would not appear in the data, and the banks would have had fewer available reserves than are indicated by the data.

To see if this possibility is a real one, let us look at the requirements for specie movements created by the distribution. While we cannot observe a gross movement of specie, such a movement was not caused by the distribution if the directives of the Secretary of the Treasury did not require it.

The total amount earmarked for distribution was $37 million. It was to be distributed in four equal installments, one at the beginning of each quarter of 1837. Only the first two installments, therefore, were distributed before specie payments were suspended, and only the first three were distributed at all. (By October 1, the government was so short of funds that it canceled the last installment.) The distribution thus did not require the movement of $37 million worth of specie; it could have required at most the movement of half this amount before the suspension of payments took place.

This upper bound is far too large to indicate the magnitude of the actual movement. The Federal Government paid its obligations in specie as a matter of policy, but it did so by giving the recipient of government funds a draft on a deposit bank. The

29. Sumner, pp. 280–81; Hammond, p. 456.

bank was obligated to give specie for the draft if requested, but
it is not clear that the states receiving the distribution insisted
on specie for the first two installments.[30] At least six states deposited the funds they received in the banks that had been the
government depositories within those states. These transactions
certainly did not require specie. Ten additional states also deposited the money they received in banks, but we do not know
what proportion of the money was transferred from one bank to
another. Most of the remaining 10 states distributed their shares
to their towns and counties, and they too were probably deposited in banks.[31]

Banks used specie to settle inter-bank differences, but it is
unlikely that a state would have forced a bank within its borders
to do so. The states were notoriously lenient toward their own
banks, and in a distribution taking place within the state, the
state surely would have favored the debtor over the creditor
bank, particularly since the creditor bank was acting on its
behalf. It is reasonable to assume, therefore, that specie was not
needed for the distribution within states, even for those states in
which the deposits were shifted from one bank to another.[32]

Specie normally was required for interregional bank settlements, and there was no reason for the administration of one
state to have urged its treasurer to be lenient toward a debtor
bank of another state. Interstate transfers have always been
implicitly emphasized in the description of the distribution, and
it is appropriate to ask about their magnitude.[33] The relevant
data appear in Table 4.4, which has been abstracted from a
Treasury compilation of the transfer drafts issued for the
actual distribution. The total interstate transactions required by

30. After the suspension, the Treasury continued to draw checks on
its deposit banks, saying, "It is therefore hoped that they will be paid in
a matter satisfactory to the holders." *Niles' Weekly Register,* LII (May
20, 1837), 177.

31. Bourne, pp. 44–124. The six states known to be using the Federal Government's deposit banks were Ala., Ky., Md., Pa., Tenn., and
Va.

32. Timberlake, 1960, p. 11.

33. Hammond, p. 456, as quoted in Chapter 1.

TABLE 4.4

Interstate Transfers in the Distribution of the Surplus, 1837
(thousands of dollars)

Location of receiving state:

DONOR STATE	NEW ENGLAND	MIDDLE ATLANTIC	SOUTH-EAST	SOUTH-WEST	NORTH-WEST	TOTAL
First Installment						
Massachusetts	250					250
New York	173	176	163			512
Pennsylvania			85			85
Louisiana				34 [ab]		34
Mississippi				216 [a]		216
Kentucky				33 [ab]		33
Ohio				33 [ab]	80	113
Indiana					114	114
TOTAL						1,357
Second Installment						
Massachusetts	177					177
New York	248	156	338	50 [b]		792
Pennsylvania			85			85
Kentucky				38 [b]		38
Ohio				38 [b]	80	118
Indiana					114	114
TOTAL						1,324
Third Installment						
New York		303	127	613		1,043
Pennsylvania		292				292
Mississippi			96			96
Kentucky		276				276
Ohio		150			60	210
Indiana					114	114
TOTAL						2,031

[a] First and Second Installments Combined.
[b] In lieu of dishonored draft from the Agricultural Bank at Natchez.
SOURCE: *U. S. Congress, House Document 30, 25th Congress, 1st Session (1837), pp. 72–81.*

the first installment amounted to only $1.4 million; those for the second, $1.3 million. This is far less than $37 million, or the half of $37 million distributed before the banks suspended payment.

Even these estimates may overstate the actual specie movements. It can be seen from Table 4.4 that the disbursements were not ordered in a random fashion. Banks in Massachusetts —meaning primarily Boston—remitted funds to other New England states; banks in New York—usually in the city as well as the state by that name—sent funds north and south along the Atlantic Coast. The smaller disbursements from other states were also to neighboring states. In the first two installments, only the disbursements from New York and the smaller ones from Pennsylvania and Ohio can be classified as interregional. Instead, most interstate transfers were from a commercial center to an outlying district. The trade of these outlying districts was channeled through the large commercial cities, and drafts on the cities were more desirable than specie (before May 10). As Biddle said, "[T]here is no individual and no state in the union that would not prefer payments in New York or the North Atlantic cities, to payments anywhere else; and for this obvious reason—that money is worth more there than anywhere else." [34]

The demand for specie stemming from the distribution of the surplus therefore was not large. In particular, the inference that the distribution placed large strains on the banks in New York must be rejected.[35] Bank drafts drawn on New York banks would not have been withdrawn in specie, and there is no evidence that the New York banks refused to honor the drafts drawn on them for the first two installments of the distribu-

34. Nicholas Biddle, Letter to J. Q. Adams, November 11, 1836. Reprinted in *Niles' Weekly Register,* LI (December 17, 1836), 243–45. See also Appleton, p. 9; Berry, p. 540.
35. Timberlake, 1960, p. 116, agreed with the conclusions presented here about the volume of interstate transfers, but asserted that "in case of interstate demands (particularly against New York) the state treasuries required specie, provoking a bank-credit contraction which in fact was the Crisis of 1837."

tion.[36] In addition, the New York banks combined together to plan a shipment of one million dollars in specie *to England* at the end of March, just before the second installment was due.[37] Had the New York banks been short of specie for the second installment, they would not have chosen this moment to plan a shipment of specie to England. They were under pressure, but the pressure did not come from the distribution.

There exists in the literature a more subtle argument about the effects of the distribution than the one we have been considering here. This argument grants all that we have asserted, but maintains that the Secretary of the Treasury, Levi Woodbury, shifted the public deposits between regions in late 1836 to avoid a large demand for specie at the actual distribution and that this shift placed intolerable strains on the banking system.[38] It will be recalled that the deposit act required public deposits in any one bank to be less than three fourths of the bank's capital. This provision necessitated large transfers of public funds, and it is not possible to separate the transfers resulting from this cause from the transfers designed to minimize the geographical movement of funds in the distribution.

In December, 1836, Congress queried the Secretary of the Treasury on the volume of transfers necessitated by the deposit act. The Secretary replied that the purposes for which transfer drafts were made were not recorded and that no one could know the proportion of these drafts issued to comply with the act. He proceeded to make an estimate from memory, however, and we can use his figure as a starting point. The total volume of transfers for all purposes between the passage of the act in June and the report in December was $25 million. In addition, there were transfer drafts amounting to $13 million outstanding, payable in the first part of 1837. The total volume of drafts ordered since the act was thus $38 million. The Secretary esti-

36. As noted in Table 4.4, the Agricultural Bank at Natchez, Miss., did not honor its drafts, but this was hardly the cause of the panic.
37. *Niles' Weekly Register*, LII (April 1, 1837), 65.
38. Biddle, Letter to J. Q. Adams, November 11, 1836, *Niles' Weekly Register*, LI, pp. 243–45; Govan, pp. 301–02; Scheiber, pp. 208–09.

mated that about $18 million had had to be transferred to
reallocate the deposits existing in June to comply with the act
and that about $12 million of the additional $22 million in
revenue that had accrued since June also had to be moved. The
total transfers due to the act were thus about $30 million, or by
far the greater part of the total $38 million.

It is clear from the Secretary's description that these transfers were caused by the provision of the act regulating the deposit banks, not by an attempt to geographically reallocate the
deposits. This intention may be seen in the nature of the
transfers issued. Only five states lost public deposits between
June 20 and December 19, 1836. Of these losses, only two
exceeded a quarter of a million dollars, and the losses from all
five states totaled just under $1.5 million. It is clear that the net
effect of the Treasury's actions was not to reallocate the government deposits among the different regions of the country.[39]

The gross volume of transfers was far greater than the net
movements suggest, and they subjected the banking system to
strain. Large government transfers, however, were not a new
phenomenon. The Bank of the United States had repaid $8.7
million in government debt on July 1, 1829, when the quantity
of money was much smaller than in 1836. And in the 10
months from June 30, 1835, to April 23, 1836, the Treasury
had transferred nearly $18 million of the public deposits. This
was a monthly volume of slightly less than half the monthly
volume of Treasury transfers in the last six months of 1836, but
the public deposits were smaller in the earlier period, and the
transfers were almost as large relative to the total volume of
public deposits as the transfers in late 1836.[40]

39. U. S. Congress, Senate Document 29, 24th Congress, 2nd Session (1836). Appendix B of this document contains a list of all the
transfers ordered between the dates cited in the text. Appendix C is a
table showing the deposits by states on the two dates. It is reproduced in
Bourne, p. 142, with some additional calculations and a few misprints.
40. N. Biddle to J. Q. Adams, November 11, 1836; Taus, p. 268;
U. S. Congress, Senate Document 356, 24th Congress, 1st Session (1836),
pp. 1–11. The government's deposits were $8 million at the end of 1834,
$26 million at the end of 1835, and $45 million at the end of 1836. The
motivation of the transfers before June, 1836, appears to have been to

But even if large governmental transactions had been un-known before 1836, could the strain produced by the transfers in that year have led to the suspension of payments in May, 1837? The answer is negative. In the first place, the banking system appeared to handle the transfers through all of 1836. Since the crisis did not come until after these transfers were completed, it is a little hard to know how they would have caused it. In the second place, the crisis appears to have cen-tered in New York and New Orleans. Public deposits in New Orleans increased by well over a million dollars in the second half of 1836, and banks in New York were making plans to send specie to England at the height of the crisis in early 1837. Neither of these cities appears to have suffered from the neces-sity to remit specie to other parts of the country. And in the third place, the volume of transfers ordered by the Treasury was not completely out of scale with transactions in other parts of the economy.

It is hard to know the total volume of transactions in any single year, but a few rough estimates may be attempted. The gross national product, into which only some transactions en-tered, was one and a half *billion* dollars in 1839.[41] The govern-ment transfers did not enter into this total as they did not generate income, but they represented a much smaller volume of transactions. Land sales alone amounted to $25 million in 1836. They also were not income-generating transactions, and they must be added to the transactions entering the gross na-tional product. They were close to the size of the governmental transfers by themselves, yet no one says that the strain of the land purchases led to the crisis. The distribution, while it posed a burden for the banking system, and while it created much trouble after the suspension of payments, did not cause the suspension.

---

shift the public deposits to the East. The effort apparently was not suc-cessful. The transfers before June, 1836, like the ones after, were largely within regions; less than $4 million had been transferred from the West to banks east of the Allegheny Mountains.

41. Gallman, 1966, p. 26.

This is not to say that the measures taken to implement the deposit act did not impose hardships on individual banks. In particular, it was noted above that two states lost over $250,000 in government deposits in the last half of 1836. One of these states was New York; its loss ($570,000) amounted to only about 5 percent of the public deposits in New York, and we may presume that the hardship was minimal. The other state was Michigan, and the loss in that state ($430,000) amounted to almost one fourth of the public deposits in Michigan. This created a great strain on the Michigan deposit banks, but the Panic of 1837 did not start or center in Michigan. This effect of the deposit act was important to the residents of Michigan, but it did not precipitate a general crisis.

Nevertheless, the accounts of specie movements in 1836 and 1837 usually draw their examples from the experience in Michigan.[42] In so doing, they are confusing the experience of one rather minor state with the experience of the country as a whole. The prevalent use of this example goes far to explain the discrepancy between the account being presented here and previous narratives. It also illustrates quite vividly the pitfalls in the use of specific examples, indicating why the use of aggregate data—rough though they may be—is a necessary part of historical investigation.

Cotton Prices and the Bank of England

The Specie Circular and the distribution of the surplus thus did not cause the Panic of 1837. Just as the veto of the Second Bank in 1832 cannot be held responsible for the inflation before 1836, the policies adopted in 1836 cannot be held responsible for the crisis that ended it. We need to uncover, therefore, the true cause of the Panic of 1837. And since the distribution was rejected as a cause of the panic in part because of the existence of a plan by the New York banks to send specie to England in

42. Gallatin, p. 31; Bourne, p. 35; Hammond (quoting Gallatin), p. 456.

March, 1837, it is natural to start the search for this explanation with a description of events in Britain.

The Bank of England was losing its specie reserves at a rapid rate in 1836. The Governor of the Bank of England believed that the specie went to the United States,[43] but it is clear from the data in Table 3.5 that the United States was not importing large quantities of gold from Britain in 1836. The Bank of England lost about £3.5 million in gold, or about $17 million. The United States, however, imported only $7 million in gold in fiscal 1836 (that is, the year ending September 30, 1836), and it was a net exporter of gold in fiscal 1837. In addition, approximately $5 million of the imports were in payment of the French indemnity, and most of that came from France. The gold that the Bank of England lost in 1836 did not go to the United States, but it is not known where it went.

In any case, the Bank of England responded to the gold outflow by raising its discount rate from 4 percent to 4.5 percent in July and to 5 percent in August. It also refused to discount bills of exchange drawn on mercantile banking houses engaged in Anglo-American trade, barring them access to its credit even at the higher rates of interest. These policies became known through the disclosure of the Bank of England's instructions to its Liverpool branch, and the credit of all persons engaged in the American trade was jeopardized.[44]

The Bank of England acted so severely and in this particular manner because it was concerned about the volume of credit outstanding in the trade with America. This concern may have been aggravated by the news of the Specie Circular, which implied to the Bank of England—as it did to most contemporaries —that the demand for specie in the United States would rise. But the Governor of the Bank of England *did not mention* the Specie Circular in his discussion of the presumed flow of specie

43. J. Horsley Palmer, *The Causes and Consequences of the Pressure upon the Money Market* (London, 1837), p. 29; Matthews, p. 93.
44. This account of events in Britain is adapted largely from Hidy, pp. 205–24.

from England to the United States in 1836, and President Jackson's measure does not seem to have affected his thinking.[45] The trade with the United States had certainly grown with unprecedented rapidity in the preceding few years, and a belief that the gold losses were going to the United States as a result of the demands of trade would have stimulated fears about the end result of providing credit for such trade. There were causes for alarm independent of the Specie Circular, and the Bank of England probably would have taken the measures it did without it.

The market rate of discount in England rose with the Bank of England's rate, and some of the merchant bankers active in the American trade began to contract their operations.[46] Baring Brothers, one of the principal houses engaged in this trade, curtailed its operations sharply. The volume of credit offered was less than half the volume extended in the previous year. New accounts were discouraged, and conditions for existing accounts were made more stringent. American importers sometimes kept accounts with several merchant bankers in England, borrowing from one to pay off the debts owed to another. Baring Brothers refused to extend credit to any importer who maintained an account with another merchant bank and insisted that new credits not be extended until old ones had been paid.

With credit hard to get, trade slowed. As the demand for goods fell, bills drawn on goods previously exported became hard to sell. By the end of February, bills drawn on three houses engaged in the American trade—one of which had already received help from the merchant banking community in December—were unsalable, and they applied to the Bank of England for help. The names of these firms (Wiggin, Wildes,

45. Palmer, pp. 29–32. See also Sir John Clapham, *The Bank of England* (Cambridge, England: Cambridge University Press, 1944), II, 150–53.

46. Matthews, pp. 57–58, 175–76, has demonstrated the existence of a close connection between the market rate of discount in England and the Bank of England's bullion reserves.

and Wilson) all began with "W," and the progress of the "three W's" was watched with considerable interest. The Bank of England permitted them to continue a restricted business under specified constraints, but they were forced to contract their operations in an effort to regain liquidity.

As a result of the English contractions, credit became hard to get in the United States; the discount rate on commercial paper in New York and Boston was above 2 percent a month in late 1836.[47] The Bank of England proposed to increase the availability of credit in the United States by offering the Bank of the United States—chartered as a state bank in Pennsylvania since March, 1836—a credit of £2 million with Baring Brothers in return for a shipment of £1 million in specie. New York bankers simultaneously petitioned the Bank of the United States for help. The Philadelphia bank responded to the appeal from New York by proposing that it and some of the appealing banks issue new bonds and that it and the New York banks each send $1 million in specie to London to cover them, at least in part. This was the planned shipment of specie that has already been referred to. The English proposal reached Philadelphia after the American plan had been formulated. It was rejected, the Bank of the United States keeping to the plan that required the smallest shipment of specie to England. The nature of these proposals to ease the financial pressure shows clearly that the pressure derived from international—not domestic—conditions.

As a result of the financial pressure, the price of cotton began to fall at the start of 1837; it was equal to the price of the previous year in January, nine tenths of the previous year's price in February and March, seven tenths of the previous year's price in April and May.[48] This decline is shown in the first column of Table 3.7 (as an annual average), and it is decomposed in the other columns. The financial crisis was peculiar to 1837, and it shows up in Table 3.7 under "other British demand," which fell sharply from 1836 to 1837. While this cate-

47. Smith and Cole, p. 192.
48. Gray, II, 1027. The New Orleans price is meant.

gory is a residual including more than the financial developments just described, there is no reason to doubt that most of the change was a result of the financial crisis.

The price of cotton, however, was not determined solely by financial conditions, and some of the other determinants also changed from 1836 to 1837. The supply of cotton—that is, the American cotton harvest—and the British price level did not change much, but the rise in the price of bread in England helped to depress the price of cotton.

The British wheat harvest was not appreciably worse in 1837 than it had been in 1836, but it was worse than the harvest in 1835 and considerably worse than the harvests of 1832 through 1834. It is likely, although not known with certainty, that the stocks of wheat in Britain increased from 1832 to 1835 as a result of the good harvests of those years and that they fell thereafter. In particular, prices were kept down during 1836 and 1837 by drawing on stocks accumulated during the previous years. Judging from the extreme reaction to the bad harvest of 1838, these stocks were running low by 1837, and the price of wheat was thereby allowed to rise. This reduced the real income of workers, and their demand for cotton goods fell. The result was a fall in the demand for cotton.[49]

Offsetting the fall in demand from the British financial crisis and poor harvest is an apparent rise in the American demand shown in Table 3.7. This observation, however, is probably spurious. The American and British prices of cotton are averages, and the periods they cover do not exactly match. The American average starts in September with the new crop, while the British average is for the calendar year.[50] The American price used to derive Table 3.7 thus lagged behind the British

49. Matthews, pp. 28–42, has a complete discussion of the harvests, stocks, and imports. On the specific years 1836 and 1837, Matthews cited Tooke, II, 257, and V, 173.

50. Gray, II, 1027; B. R. Mitchell and Phyllis Deane, *Abstract of British Historical Statistics* (Cambridge, England: Cambridge University Press, 1962), p. 491. The American price for 1837 would have been 15 percent lower if it had been a calendar-year average.

price for reasons having nothing to do with the events of 1837. In a period of falling prices like 1837, this lag raised the ratio of the American to the British price, a rise which appears in Table 3.7 as an increase in American demand.[51] (Similarly the low American demand in 1838 when prices were rising is in part spurious.)

The fall in the price of cotton was one of principal ways in which the pressure exerted by the Bank of England on the English financial market was communicated to the United States. As a result of this fall, debts secured by cotton became uncollectible, merchants holding such debt failed, banks found their assets illusory or at least illiquid, and they refused to honor their liabilities. In short, they suspended payment. The restrictions of the Bank of England, acting strongly through the price of cotton, bear much of the responsibility for the suspension.

The first failure attributed to the "money pressure" occurred in March, 1837. The pressure had started several months before, and it was reported as continuing "with unabated force" in the middle of that month. New York and Philadelphia firms withstood the pressure, but a New Orleans cotton factor, Herman, Briggs & Co., failed. Herman, Briggs & Co. had liabilities of $4 to $8 million, and one of its creditors, J. L. & S. Joseph & Co. of New York, "under acceptances from the New Orleans house," stopped payment. The presumption was that Joseph & Co. would fail because of difficulty with the cotton factor.[52]

A Buffalo bank was run upon by a broker and suspended later in March, and the appeal by the New York banks to the Bank of the United States was reported on the first of April. The first report of the agreement said that both the New York banks and the Bank of the United States would send one million dollars in specie to London, but a more complete account one week later said only that the Bank of the United States was to

51. See also Smith, p. 77.
52. *Niles' Weekly Register,* LII (March 3 and 18, 1837), 33, 49. The following account of events in 1837 is taken from *ibid.,* LII (April-June, 1837).

do so. The New York banks were to raise loans and discounts, issue bonds, and draw on Rothschild's in Paris, but they were not to send specie to England; their plan to sustain themselves by remitting specie had been superseded by Biddle's grand plan. As Biddle explained it in his famous letter to John A. Steven, March 29, 1837: "In the meantime what my own observations suggest as the cause of these troubles, is, that recent events in the south and in Europe, have, in concurrence with reasons of an earlier date, produced a paralysis of private credit which deranges the whole system of our foreign and domestic exchanges. For this the appropriate remedy seems to be to substitute for the private credit of individuals the more known and established credit of the bank, until public confidence in private stability has time to revive." Had the crisis been caused by a need for specie for domestic transactions, the New York banks would not have sought a remedy such as this. They would have petitioned the Bank of the United States to give them specie, not to send it abroad.

Interest rates stayed at 2 percent a month, confidence was low, brokers were failing, and banks would not discount bills from the South or West throughout March and April. Merchants could not meet their obligations as a result, and a cumulative contraction reminiscent of a banking panic was well underway. As merchants failed, bills drawn on them became worthless. As more bills lost their value, new bills became harder to sell. As credit became ever harder to find, still more merchants failed.

The failure of the Josephs was widely regarded as the start of the crisis; it was followed by the failure of other houses that dealt in bills from the South and West and by trouble among those concerned with the trade in dry goods. The New York *Journal of Commerce* reported on April 8 that the failures to date had included:

> 5 foreign and exchange brokers, with capital of $15 million,
> 30 dry goods jobbers, with capital of $15 million,
> 16 commission shoe and clothing houses, with $7 million capital,

28 real estate speculators, with $20 million capital,
8 stock brokers, with $1 million capital, and
6 miscellaneous houses, with capital of $2.5 million.

This made a total of 93 firms with an aggregate capital of $60.5 million. Yet among all these failures in New York, the *Journal of Commerce* did not report one bank.

Reports of bank troubles began to appear late in April. A Boston bank stopped payment on the 12th, Mobile banks talked of suspension, and New Orleans banks agreed to clear notes with each other. The measure in New Orleans was a cooperative effort to contain the pressure on any one bank and to regulate themselves at the same time. By clearing notes among themselves instead of using specie, they did not allow one of their number to draw down the specie reserves of the others. By acting together instead of separately, they were able to observe the relations of each bank with all other banks and thus to observe any weakness at an early stage. The similarity with the procedures adopted later in Boston is striking.[53]

The New Orleans correspondent of the *New York Courier and Enquirer* reported in a dispatch dated April 16, that "it can no longer be concealed that the commercial community at New Orleans is altogether in a complete state of bankruptcy or suspension." Ten to 12 of the first-rate houses, 40 to 50 of the second-rate houses, and one fourth of the bank directors in that city had become insolvent or stopped payment. "Merchants have no confidence in each other, and banks distrust their rivals." All this in spite of the attempt at joint action by the banks.

As April turned into May, the pressure and the failures of brokers continued, and *Niles' Weekly Register* carried the news on the 13th that banks in New York, Philadelphia, and Baltimore had suspended payments. The news was accompanied by the following comment: "It is the unavoidable result of the diversion of specie to the west, and the drain upon the banks in the Atlantic cities for exportation to Europe." There is no evi-

53. See first section of this chapter.

dence of a "diversion of specie" to the West; the suspension was due to the crisis in international trade. The extent of the crisis in New Orleans and the high incidence of failures among merchants and brokers confirm this hypothesis.

Since the problem originated in international affairs and was communicated through the cotton market, the pressure was felt first in the principal markets for cotton, New Orleans and New York. Had the pressure originated with the Specie Circular or the distribution of the surplus, the pressure would have been concentrated at first in the West or in New York, the city most drawn upon for interstate transfers, and not in New Orleans, where bank deposits of the Federal Government doubled in late 1836 and only small interstate transfers were demanded.[54] Therefore, only if the problem had originated in the cotton market would we have observed a crisis centering in New Orleans.

Similarly, since the problem originated in international trade, the financial pressure was strongest among merchants, brokers, and factors rather than among banks. If the crisis had originated with the government's actions, the pressure would have been felt first by banks. Banks would have refused to extend credit to merchants and brokers, of course, and both types of institutions would have been under pressure in any case. Reports of distress among merchants and brokers therefore may have indicated either a problem in the trade sector or efficiency on the part of banks in shifting the pressure to their debtors. It is unlikely, however, that the banks were able to transfer the pressure to others sufficiently rapidly for them to feel the pressure before the banks, and the evidence of difficulty among non-bank institutions confirms the influence of the Bank of England and the price of cotton.

The demand for specie to export, however, raises a problem of some interest. The demand rose because the sales of cotton could not cover the bills drawn on them as prices fell—that is,

54. Table 4.4; U. S. Congress, Senate Document 29, 24th Congress, 2nd Session (1836), Appendix C.

because American exports to Britain were not sufficient to cover the debts the British wished repaid. The price of a commodity in high demand normally will rise, and the price of foreign exchange rose in late 1836 when the crisis began. The exchange rate went to a premium between 2 and 3 percent over gold par in the last quarter of 1836, and it stayed there through the first quarter of 1837. It was almost—but not quite—cheaper to ship specie to England than to buy pounds with dollars, and not much specie was shipped.

The premium on pounds stayed under 3 percent through the first quarter of 1837, and when it rose above that point in the second quarter, banks suspended payment. In other words, when the price of foreign exchange rose to the point where it was profitable to buy specie and ship it to England, the banks allowed the price of specie in the United States to rise to the point where this was no longer so. The result, as shown in Table 3.5, was that only $2 million in specie was sent to England in fiscal 1837.[55]

W. B. Smith, in his analysis of the Second Bank, attached great significance to the smallness of the specie flow. He said: "The decline in the price of cotton was not sufficient to induce a net specie outflow. It can hardly have been the primary cause of the panic of 1837." [56] Given the exchange rate, there was no reason for the flow of specie to England to have been larger than it was; the banks suspended payment as an alternative to sending specie. But while the shipment of specie was appropriate to the price of foreign exchange, it still must be asked why the exchange rate acted as it did. We can rephrase Smith's observation as a question: Why didn't the premium on foreign exchange rise above 2 or 3 percent before the second quarter of 1837?

The crisis began in the fall of 1836, when the price of

55. Davis and Hughes, Table A-2; Smith and Cole, p. 190. Smith and Cole's monthly data on the price of bills of exchange show rises in the premium in April and June of 1837 of about 2 percent each, followed by a rise of 5 percent in July.
56. Smith, p. 191.

foreign exchange rose to, but not above, the specie point. Discount rates on commercial paper in New York and Boston rose to 2 or 3 percent a month at the same time. These rates were maintained for about six months, only after which the crisis turned into a panic. At that point the price of foreign exchange rose further and the banks suspended payment, but the six-month delay poses the problem.

The crisis, it is apparent, came in two stages. In the late summer of 1836 the Bank of England raised its discount rate and imposed restrictions on the availability of credit. This pressure was communicated to the United States, where it was reflected in a rise in the interest rate and the price of foreign exchange. The hardships created by these restrictions apparently were bearable as long as the price of cotton was not affected.[57]

The price of cotton continued high until the beginning of 1837, but it fell thereafter, creating additional pressure in the American money market. By May the pressure had become panic, and banks suspended payments. The crisis lasted as long as it did because the price of cotton reacted only with a lag to the restrictions on credit imposed by the Bank of England. Smith was therefore right when he said that the fall in the price of cotton was not the primary cause of the crisis. The primary cause was the action of the Bank of England, but this action made itself felt partly through its effect on the price of cotton. It is a peculiarity of the antebellum financial structure that in a time of very flexible prices, many of the credit arrangements depended on the movements of a single price.[58]

We have mentioned the actions of the American Administration only briefly in this discussion. But the Specie Circular was prominent in the thoughts of most observers in early 1837. It

57. The Bank of England could not restrict credit too much in the fall of 1836 without impeding the sale of the British harvest. Only in the spring of 1837 could it tighten up further, a move symbolized by the failure of the "three W's." I am indebted to Maurice Levy-Leboyer for this point.

58. Smith, p. 32, also observed this phenomenon.

may have helped to induce the Bank of England to act as it did. It may have induced banks in the United States to contract more severely than they might otherwise have done. It certainly increased the tension among members of the financial community. The Specie Circular was thus a factor in the crisis due to its effect on people's minds—not their finances. It has been shown that there was ample cause for a panic without the Circular, but it is not possible to assert with finality that one would have occurred without it.

Contemporary observers did not view the distribution of the surplus with as much alarm as the Specie Circular, and the case for it as a cause of the panic is accordingly weaker. On the other hand, the distribution was enormously complicated by the suspension of payments, and the histories of the two events are connected. The payment of the third installment was made after the banks had suspended payment. The government wished to pay in specie or its equivalent as it had always done, but it was not able. The Treasury said that it would continue to draw on the deposit banks—it had no choice—and that the states should not accept anything but specie. The states, however, preferred depreciated currency over a promise of specie sometime in the future, and no protest by a state unable to get specie is recorded.[59] The fourth installment fell due after payments had been suspended for some months. The government did not have the funds to pay it, and it was never paid.[60]

59. Bourne, pp. 39–40.
60. U. S. Treasury, *Report on Finances,* September, 1837, p. 3. An act of October 14, 1837, prohibited the recall of the deposits with the states. U. S. Treasury, *Report on Finances,* December, 1837, p. 2.

5

The Crisis of 1839 and the End of the Boom

Recovery and a New Crisis

The Panic of 1837 was indeed dramatic, but its effects, as we noted at the beginning of Chapter 4, were not disastrous. To discover the causes leading to the renewed expansion of 1838, the new crisis of 1839, and the following deflation, we must follow the economy through Van Buren's Administration.

Prices fell in the first part of 1837. The price of cotton had started to fall early in the year, and other prices followed as the crisis deepened. They did not fall far, however, and they began to recover toward the end of 1837. They rose somewhat unevenly throughout 1838 and peaked in the spring of 1839, banks having resumed payment in 1838. Some observers believed that the effects of the crisis were over, but the new prosperity was short-lived. Banks south and west of New York suspended payment late in 1839, and prices fell by almost one half in the next four years.[1] We seek to explain the nature of both the recovery in 1838–39 and the massive deflation that followed it.

American banks refused to redeem their obligations at par for roughly a year after the Panic of 1837. The New York banks resumed under pressure of law just before a year had passed, and banks in Philadelphia followed them in the fall of 1838 (fiscal 1838). The price of cotton stayed low throughout this year of suspended payments. The 1837 cotton crop had been unusually large, and the demand from American consumers was

1. Table 3.2.

very small, due to the crisis. (Part of the low American demand shown in Table 3.7, however, is due to the dating of the price indexes.) As a result, the price of cotton was low despite strong English demand. The poor harvest in Britain had depressed the demand from that country, but the end of the financial crisis brought financial ease and greater demand. The Bank of England's reserves increased from £ 4 million at the start of 1837 to £ 10 million at the start of 1838, and the discount rate fell accordingly. The average market rate of discount in England, which had been at 5.5 percent in the first quarter of 1837, was below 3 percent for the middle two quarters of 1838.[2]

Because the quantity of cotton exported had risen as the price fell, foreign-exchange earnings from the export of cotton did not fall in 1838. American imports were low due to the rise in the effective exchange rate during the suspension, and the American trade balance greatly improved.[3] British willingness to invest in America had not been diminished by the crisis, and the return of easy credit to that country brought a demand for American securities. As few funds were needed to finance British exports to the United States, the demand for American securities unrelated to trade was high. The several states responded to this demand, and the British market was filled with "American Stocks of Every Description" by the end of 1837.

The exchange rate between pounds and dollars fell back toward the gold par as a result of the British demand for dollars, and it became possible for the American banks to reestablish the parity between specie and bank obligations. The Bank of England aided the movement toward resumption of specie payments by shipping one million pounds in gold to New York in the spring of 1838. This gold rapidly disappeared into bank reserves and helped to ease resumption.[4]

2. Matthews, pp. 199, 201.
3. *U. S. Historical Statistics*, p. 547; North, 1960, p. 605. See Chapter 4, above.
4. Hidy, pp. 237, 244–45. The total shipment of gold from Britain to the United States in fiscal 1838 was $9 million; this single shipment amounted to over half of that. See Table 3.5.

With the United States once more on a specie standard, all seemed to be well. The British financed a large American trade deficit, the price of cotton revived, and the effects of the distribution made themselves felt. The capital flow had promoted the resumption of specie payments, but the rise in the price of cotton and the effects of the distribution were largely independent of the resumption, and they deserve separate treatment.

There were two reasons for the rise in the price of cotton in 1839. In the first place, the 1838 cotton crop was very poor. In the second, the Bank of the United States, now chartered by Pennsylvania, stepped into the void created by the failure of many cotton brokers in 1837. Technically, this was a venture by Biddle, not the Bank, but the Bank could not and did not remain distinct from this venture by its president. The motives for this venture are not altogether clear; some historians say that Biddle was trying altruistically to raise the price of cotton, and others, that he was expanding his business to replace the lost business of the Federal Government.[5] In any case, his attempts to purchase cotton helped to raise its price.

The relative effects of Biddle's actions and the short crop may be inferred from Table 3.7. In 1838, when conditions had been bad and the harvest large, the demand from American sources was small. In 1839, when financial conditions had revived and the crop was small, the American demand was high. In 1840, when the harvest once again was bountiful, the American demand once again was small. Biddle's actions acted to intensify the price fluctuations caused by the variation in the harvest, but they were effective only in conjunction with other inflationary forces. More importantly, as the subsequent story will show, they could not withstand opposing pressures. Biddle must be accounted lucky rather than successful in his 1839 cotton speculations.

The price of cotton was important as a symbol and as a part of the international credit structure, but a rise in this price did not indicate a rise in revenue. The price of cotton rose at least

5. Smith, pp. 195–202; Hammond, pp. 467–71; Matthews, p. 62.

partly because the volume of cotton exports fell, and the earnings from the crop were quite stable. The rise in the price thus did not directly draw British resources to the United States, although it helped to restore the financial system and thus investment.[6] The response of the states to the distribution of the surplus, although less noticed by historians, was of more importance to the level of income in the United States.

The Federal Government had acquired its surplus as a result of selling land. It had withdrawn funds from the private sector and held them idle, exerting a depressing effect on demand. The level of demand was so high in 1835–36 that this action did not decrease income; it only slowed the rate of inflation, as was noted in Chapter 3. In 1838 and 1839, however, after these funds were transferred from the Federal Government to the states, the states did not hold them idle. The state expenditures came at a time of relatively low demand, and they had the effect of raising income. Many states initiated new projects with their share of the surplus, typically for schools or internal improvements, and many others distributed their share to their towns or counties who may be presumed to have acted similarly.[7]

The recession of 1837–38, therefore, was brought to a speedy end by the restoration of the capital flow from Britain to the United States and by the expansion of demand stemming from the rise in state government expenditures. The rise in the price of cotton stemming from the short harvest of 1838 and Biddle's cotton speculations symbolized the recovery to contemporary observers, but its importance lay primarily in the help it provided for the restoration of the pre-1837 credit structure.

6. The value of cotton exports was between $61 and $64 million for fiscal years 1837 through 1840. *U. S. Historical Statistics*, p. 547.

7. Bourne, pp. 44–124, 132–34. Of the 26 states, 5 spent their share on schools, 4 spent it on internal improvements, 4 more distributed it to towns or counties. We do not know about the others. Expenditures by states were at their peak in 1838 and 1839 in the North. They had begun to decline from their peak (around 1837) in the South. Lance E. Davis and John Legler, "The Government in the American Economy, 1815–1902: A Quantitative Study," *Journal of Economic History*, XXVI (December, 1966), 532–33.

Since the banks resumed specie payments and the British began to export capital again before the price rise, it can be doubted how important it was. On the other hand, had the price of cotton not risen, the Bank of the United States might have failed in 1839 instead of 1841, and this could have prevented the British lending, and possibly also the American economy, from recovering.

The economy did recover, but the prosperity was short-lived. There is no single cause of the crisis in 1839, and the causes must be sought in the dislocations of trade and finance that started in 1837. The analysis of the proximate causes of the new crisis will make the connections with earlier events clear.

The British wheat harvest in 1838 was very poor. Imports of wheat to Britain consequently were very large in 1839, and the bullion reserves of the Bank of England declined precipitously as a result. The reserves, which had stood at £10 million at the start of 1838, fell below £3 million in the third quarter of 1839. The English discount rate responded to the resultant monetary pressure by rising from less than 3 percent in the middle of 1838 to 6 percent and over in the second half of 1839.[8]

As in 1837, the demand for cotton and the supply of capital for the United States both decreased. The fall in the British demand for cotton was already noticeable in the months when other influences kept the price high, and it ensured that when these other supports were removed, the price would fall. The decreasing supply of exportable capital did not make itself felt until the start of fiscal 1840—that is, until autumn of 1839—but capital imports to the United States decreased by $80 million from fiscal 1839 to fiscal 1840. This was much larger than the fall from fiscal 1837 to fiscal 1838, which had been about $20 million, and it was bound to have a larger effect. It was equal to about 5 percent of the American national product,

8. Matthews, pp. 94, 199, 201.

larger than the total expenditures on railroads and canals of about 2 percent.[9]

This fall in capital imports can be seen also as a rise in capital exports. In fact, the United States was a net exporter of capital in 1840 for the first time since 1830. Unless the national product increased from 1839 to 1840, the increase in capital exports must have come from a corresponding decrease in domestic investment or in consumption. The data on these aggregate quantities are not of the best, but it appears that domestic investment fell.[10]

The state projects initiated in the late 1830's had been started in the expectations of external financing. Capital imports and the distribution of the Federal Government's surplus initially had confirmed the expectation that resources were freely available. The decline in capital imports in fiscal 1838 was offset by the effects of the distribution and did not alter these expectations. The resumption of capital imports in the next year appeared to justify continued optimism. Unfortunately, the new inflow of foreign capital did not continue, and the decline thereafter had neither offsets nor reversals. Unbounded optimism was replaced by its opposite, and the manifold projects of the states were abandoned.

As this turnabout in the American balance of payments was beginning to develop, a bumper crop of cotton was brought in. The crop of 1839 was fully one half again as large as the short crop of 1838, and the price of cotton fell as its magnitude became known. The price started its decline in the fall of 1839, and Biddle's efforts to sustain it collapsed. The large harvest

9. North, 1960, p. 621; Gallman, 1966, p. 26, and private correspondence. British capital exports fell by £5.4 million, or less than $30 million, indicating that capital exports to the United States from other countries fell also, or that North's data exaggerate the fall. Mitchell and Deane, p. 333.

10. Gallman, private correspondence. Consumption, domestic investment, and foreign investment were estimated separately, and the estimates may not reveal all their interconnections.

and the low American demand produced a sharp swing in the price of cotton, even though the British demand did not change. The discount rate on commercial bills rose to the crisis levels of late 1836 and early 1837. The Bank of the United States, caught by the falling price and the results of many ill-fated decisions made when the price was high, suspended payments for the second time in October, 1839. Its example was followed to the South and West, but banks in New York and New England did not suspend.[11]

The crisis of 1839 was brief; like the Panic of 1837, it did not outlast the suspension of specie payments. It was not as severe as the earlier panic—there was no scarcity of foreign exchange and not all banks suspended payments. Yet, unlike 1837, no recovery followed the panic in 1839. Prices did not recover, and the signs of prosperity disappeared. Nine states found themselves unable to pay the interest due on their bonds in 1841 and 1842 and defaulted. Europeans decided that American state bonds were not as good an investment as they had seemed, and the capital flow to America ceased.[12] Either prices or incomes in the United States had to fall to reduce the American demand for imports to the point where imports could be paid for by exports. We shall ask whether it was prices or incomes that fell, but in either case, the boom was over.

The role of the Bank of the United States in precipitating this second crisis has been debated at length. Biddle maintained that the Bank was blameless, but opponents of this view have not been lacking.[13] It can be seen from the foregoing tale that the forces ending the boom were independent of the Bank, much as the forces initiating it had been. The Bank may have

11. Smith and Cole, p. 190; Smith, pp. 210–19.
12. Ratchford, pp. 98, 101. The 9 states were Fla., Miss., Ark., Ind., Ill., Md., Mich., Pa., La. The first four defaulted in 1841; the others, in 1842.
13. "It may be affirmed in this respect that the bank, subsequent to the first general suspension of May, 1837, has been the principal, if not the sole, cause of the delay in resuming and of subsequent suspensions. In every respect it has been a public nuisance." Gallatin, p. 45.

played a role in the re-establishment of American credit abroad in 1837 and 1838. If so, its subsequent actions may have brought on the panic in 1839 by jeopardizing that credit. This hypothesis, however, implies that the alternative to a crisis in 1839 was continued depression in 1838, and it is not clear that this alternative was preferable.

The Bank of the United States finally failed in 1841, after resuming payments for only a few weeks. Its directors and officers must take blame for its demise, but they cannot be held responsible for the depression in which it failed. The political importance of the Bank of the United States had far outweighed the economic.

Deflation or Depression?

There was no recovery in 1839 or 1840, and prices fell 46 percent from their peak in February, 1839, to a trough in February, 1843.[14] Bank failures multiplied; the brave projects started in the 1830's were abandoned or deferred to better times; and gloom settled upon contemporary observers.

This deflation is often compared to the events from 1929 to 1933. Hammond drew a parallel between the events of the late 1830's and "a similar crisis ninety-six years later" to contrast the policies of Roosevelt and Van Buren. North, in his analysis of the antebellum economy, said, "The period from the fall of 1839 to 1843 resembles a similar era just ninety years later in that both were severe and prolonged drops in economic activity." And Friedman and Schwartz, writing about the 20th century, said, "To find anything in our history remotely comparable to the monetary collapse from 1929 to 1933, one must go back nearly a century to the contraction of 1839 to 1843." [15] There was a sharp price decline in both periods; the financial

14. Table 3.2. Prices stopped falling in late 1840, but they resumed their fall in 1842.
15. Hammond, p. 529; North, 1961, p. 202; Friedman and Schwartz, p. 299.

system in both cases was in acute distress. But the comparison seems to imply more than this. It suggests that the decline in production that was such a prominent part of the early 1930's was also paralleled in the 1840's.

It is possible that the deflation of the early 1840's was accompanied by a major depression, but it is also possible that it was not. The economy was very different in the two periods, and falling prices may have *substituted* for falling production in the early 19th century. Although demand was lower in the early 1840's than in the late 1830's, the same quantities could have been demanded at a lower price. Prices could have fallen because the supply of money fell. The reports of unemployment that we have from 1837 and 1839 may have been responses to the crises of those years; the unemployment of 1839 could have been as transitory as that of 1837. It is not possible to show from a consideration of price data alone that the deflation of the early 1840's was accompanied by a depression like the one of the 1930's.

An explicit comparison of 1839–43 and 1929–33 is presented in Table 5.1. The top three rows of the table show the changes in a few monetary variables during these periods. The supply of money and prices both fell further in the 19th-century contraction, but a greater percentage of the nation's banks failed in the later decline. The two periods appear quite comparable on the basis of these monetary measures.

The lower three rows in Table 5.1 show changes in real magnitudes during the two periods.[16] The parallels that showed so prominently in the first three rows of the table are not apparent here. Gross investment virtually disappeared in 1933, but it declined by less than one quarter from 1839 to 1843. Consumption, which fell by one fifth in the early 1930's actually rose in the early 1840's. The gross national product, which is

16. The data for 1839–43 are presented in 1860 prices; those for 1929–33, in 1954 prices. Although they are not strictly comparable for this reason, they both give the changes in terms of prices about 20 years after the depression started.

TABLE 5.1

Comparison of 1839–43 with 1929–33 (percent)

	1839–43	1929–33
Change in money stock	—34	—27
Change in prices	—42	—31
Change in number of banks	—23	—42
Change in real gross investment	—23	—91
Change in real consumption	+21	—19
Change in real gross national product	+16	—30

NOTES: The 1839–43 data are taken from peak to trough of the respective series, and dates differ somewhat. Data on money and banks are from late 1838 to late 1842; data on prices, from calendar-year 1839 to calendar-year 1843; data on G.N.P., etc., from census-year 1839 (year ending May 31, 1839) to census-year 1843.
SOURCES:
1839–43: Tables 3.2, 3.3, 5.2; Gallman, private correspondence; U. S. Historical Statistics, p. 624.
1929–33: Ibid., pp. 116, 143, 624, 646.

the sum of investment and consumption, rose in the early 1840's and fell in the early 1930's.

If these data are correct, it is clear that the parallel between the two periods is limited. The deflation was severe in both cases, but only one was a major depression. Investment was down in the 1840's, but the flow of goods and services to consumers did not fall. It did not even seem to slow its growth, and we can infer from this that discomfort was not widespread. The economy appears to have been one in which prices could change by large amounts without upsetting production.[17]

17. The author of these estimates of G.N.P. and its components in the 1840's emphasized that the annual data were derived only "to reduce our dependence on benchmark year estimates." They were not intended to be used for analyses of yearly changes, and they may not be appropriate for such use. If they are to reduce our dependence on benchmark-year estimates in any meaningful sense, however, they must also reflect the conditions of the economy in the intervening years, and we are not amiss if we use them to discover these conditions. See Gallman, 1966, pp. 64–71.

It was shown in Chapter 3 that prices responded to changes in the supply of money. When the supply of money rose in the mid-1830's, the demand for goods increased. Both the production and the prices of goods rose in response to this higher demand, but prices rose for more than production. Similarly, the supply of money fell rapidly in the early 1840's decreasing the demand for goods. Prices fell, but the production of goods continued to grow.

The supply of money was a function of the stock of specie, the reserve ratio of banks, and the proportion of money the public wished to hold in specie (coin). These magnitudes are shown in Table 5.2, which continues the series in Table 3.3. The amount of specie in the United States did not change much in the early 1840's. After the panics of the later 1830's, however, banks increased their reserve ratios from under 20 percent to over 30 percent, and this action was echoed by the actions of individuals. Having discovered that bank obligations were not always as good as specie, the public desired to hold far more specie than it had held in the 1830's. The proportion of money held as specie had been rising in the late 1830's, and it reached a peak of 35 percent late in 1842. As banks and individuals demanded more specie relative to bank obligations, the amount of bank obligations a given amount of specie could support fell. The supply of money fell, and prices fell to clear the market. A radical increase in the supply of money and a slow rise in the availability of goods to buy with it had produced inflation in the 1830's; a rapid fall in the supply of money coupled with an increase in the production of goods produced the deflation of the 1840's.

It emerged in Chapter 3 that prices rose in the 1830's because production could not. The productive resources of the economy were already fully employed at the start of the boom, and there was no way for them to be increased rapidly enough to satisfy the increased demand arising from the rapid rise in the supply of money. There was no corresponding barrier to a fall in production in the 1840's, and we must ask why the fall in demand deriving from the decline in the supply of money was

TABLE 5.2

The Supply of Money and Its Determinants, 1840–58

END OF YEAR	MONEY	SPECIE	RESERVE RATIO	PROPORTION OF MONEY HELD AS SPECIE
	($ million)	($ million)	(percent)	(percent)
1840	186	80	25	24
1841	174	80	23	30
1842	158	90	33	35
1843	194	100	35	26
1844	214	96	27	24
1845	241	97	23	23
1846	267	120	19	32
1847	281	112	21	23
1848	267	120	23	28
1849	329	154	20	33
1850	399	186	19	34
1851	N.A.	204	N.A.	N.A.
1852	451	236	18	42
1853	546	241	16	33
1854	539	250	16	36
1855	565	250	16	34
1856	611	260	14	33
1857	498	260	24	37
1858	569	250	25	25

N.A. = Not Available.
SOURCES: *See Appendix. An alternate estimate of the value of specie in the United States is presented there.*

reflected in a fall in prices rather than unemployment and a fall in production.

There is no compelling *a priori* reason why this should have been so: People could have become unemployed, for example, had prices been rigid and incapable of falling. Each economy reacts differently to a fall in demand, and it is necessary to describe the economy of the 1840's to see why prices fell more than production. Most 19th-century economists thought that a fall in demand would always result in a fall in prices rather than production. This classical view of the economy is not appropriate to the 20th century, and this is not the place to test its validity for the 19th century as a whole. Yet to the extent that the events of the 1840's agree with the predictions of the classical economists, they provide evidence of the relevance of classical theories to the world in which classical economists lived.

The major part of production in the 1840's was for consumption, and about half of the consumption goods were agricultural. We saw in Chapter 3 that the supply of cotton was independent of its price; the size of the crop was determined by the size of the available labor force and the weather. We do not know the supply functions of other crops, but if cotton—the most commercialized of all antebellum crops—was supplied inelastically, the sum of all crops probably was too. Farmers were aware of prices and raised crops for sale, but they had no alternative to farming. When the price of their crops fell, the incentive to reduce production because of its decreased profitability was balanced by the need to produce more to preserve their former income. And if other prices fell also, as they did in the 1840's, the farmer would have less incentive to change his ways than if the price of his crop alone had fallen. The United States Patent Office collected data on crops during the 1840's, and the data show no drop in production in the early years of the decade.[18]

The other half of consumption was composed of manufactured goods and services, about which we know much less than

18. Robert E. Gallman, "A Note on the Patent Office Crop Estimates, 1841–1848," *Journal of Economic History,* XXIII (June, 1963), 192.

There is some evidence that agricultural prices, at least in the West, fell more sharply than industrial prices in the early 1840's (Berry, p. 125). This observation suggests that the fall in demand had different consequences in the agricultural and industrial sectors. In agriculture, output was maintained, and the fall in demand lowered prices. In industry, output was restricted in response to the fall in demand, and prices consequently did not fall as far as they would have had production not fallen. The evidence of the cotton-textile industry does not bear out this suggestion, but the behavior of those industries for which data have survived may not have been typical of industry as a whole. I am indebted to Robert Shiller for this point.

we do about agriculture. Just as the largest single crop was cotton, the largest single industry was the cotton-textile industry. Most of the reports of unemployment in the late 1830's came from cotton-textile centers in New England, and the condition of this industry has been regarded as symptomatic of industry in general. The reports of unemployment, however, come from the crisis years 1837 and 1839; they do not tell us about conditions in the early 1840's. Two estimates of the cotton-textile industry's output have been made recently. They differ on many counts, including the method of derivation, but they both fail to show a sustained decline in production in the early 1840's. In fact, the production in 1843 was shown to be about 15 percent above the 1839 level in both estimates.[19]

This does not mean that profits were stable in the 1840's; the profits of a sample of cotton-textile firms fell from 14 percent in 1839 to 2 percent in 1843. Two reasons have been given for the failure of output to follow profits. The minimum cost of production was reached when the mills were running at their top speed for the daylight hours—that is, when they were running at full capacity. Cotton mills were operated as a result either at full speed or not at all, and output stayed close to capacity. Further, although additions to capacity were made in response to high profits, the process took time, and new capacity did not become available until after profits had started to decline. Output, consequently, did not fall when profits did.[20]

There is no way of knowing if the cotton-textile industry was typical of industry in general, but data on trade support the contention that production did not fall. Trade, of course, in-

19. Rezneck compiled contemporary reports of unemployment. For the estimates of cotton-textile production, see Lance E. Davis and H. Louis Stettler, III, "The New England Textile Industry, 1825–60: Trends and Fluctuations," in *Output, Employment, and Productivity in the United States after 1800*, Studies in Income and Wealth, Vol. 30 (New York: Columbia University Press for the National Bureau of Economic Research, 1966), p. 221; Zevin.

20. McGouldrick, pp. 9, 12–13, 29, 81. Despite these conclusions, the output of firms in McGouldrick's sample did not rise between 1839 and 1843. *Ibid.*, p. 142. See the further discussion of this point below.

cluded agricultural as well as industrial goods, and the data may
reflect more the maintenance of production on the farm rather
than in the factory. Nevertheless, the tonnages passing through
New York State canals and the real volume of exports did not
decline for more than one or two years during the late 1830's
and early 1840's. Imports, of course, did fall, and people deriving their income from the sale or financing of imports were
hurt.[21]

Investment, as can be seen in Table 5.1, was a different
story. Railroad construction fell by two thirds from its peak in
1838 to its trough in 1843, and canal construction fell by nine
tenths from its peak in 1839 to its trough in 1834. These falls
are comparable to the decline in total investment in the 1930's,
but they apply only to a small part of investment in the 1840's.
Railroad and canal investment together were less than one fifth
of total investment in 1839 and less than one twentieth in
1843.[22]

The rest of investment was composed of farm construction,
residential construction and industrial investment. Farm construction constituted almost half of all investment in the decade
from 1834 to 1843. Since agricultural production did not cease
its expansion, agricultural investment undoubtedly did not fall.
Residential construction, to the extent we know about it, also
did not fall in the early 1840's.[23] Industrial investment, however, presented a mixed picture. Investment in cotton-textile

21. *U. S. Historical Statistics,* p. 455; North, 1961, pp. 89–91, 241–
43. Smith and Cole's index of trade cannot be used to indicate the
volume of trade as it includes items like the value of imports and the
volume of redemptions at the Suffolk Bank in Boston which varied
with the price level as well as the volume of trade. See Smith and Cole,
pp. 70–73. Trade on some Western canals did fall, however, even though
agricultural production did not. See James Hall, *The West; Its Commerce and Navigation* (Cincinnati, 1848), p. 81.

22. Gallman, private correspondence.

23. On farm construction, see Gallman, 1966, p. 15. For residential
construction, see Gottlieb, who said, p. 81, of his data that they can
"lay out only the general course of residential building within these
decades." Manuel Gottlieb, *Estimates of Residential Building, 1840–
1939* (National Bureau of Economic Research Technical Paper 17)
(New York: National Bureau of Economic Research, 1964), p. 81.

mills fell dramatically in response to the continuance of low profits after 1839 while investment in the iron industry remained relatively strong.

The only direct study of investment in the cotton-textile industry showed that investment was a function of profit and that when profits fell in the late 1830's and early 1840's, investment fell also. This should have produced a slower growth of capacity and hence of output, but—as we have already noted—output continued to grow during the early 1840's. The author of the investment study asserted that this was due to lags in the response of investment to profits, but it is unlikely that the lag was longer than the period of low profits in the early 1840's. More probably, this discrepancy must stand as a still unresolved difference between the available sources.[24]

New blast furnaces were being built throughout the 1830's, and their number increased by half during that decade. Almost all of these blast furnaces were a traditional type that used charcoal for fuel. In the early 1840's the construction of furnaces using charcoal for fuel almost ceased; the number of these furnaces increased by less than 5 percent from 1839 to 1843. On the other hand, a new and more efficient type of furnace had just been introduced, one which used anthracite coal for fuel. Construction of this type of blast furnace did not abate during the early 1840's, and the capacity of all blast furnaces, measured in the tons of pig iron that could be produced, rose by 20 percent from 1839 to 1843. This rate of growth is slower than the rates in surrounding years, but it indicates a slowing of growth, not a cessation or decline of production. The low level of demand thus hurt the traditional, inefficient sector of the industry, but it did not extend to the newer furnaces. Even though some of the anthracite-using furnaces replaced older ones, net investment in the iron industry was still substantial in the early 1840's.[25]

24. McGouldrick, pp. 159, 189, and references cited above on cotton-textile production.

25. Peter Temin, *Iron and Steel in Nineteenth-Century America: An Economic Inquiry* (Cambridge: M.I.T. Press, 1964), pp. 61, 236–

The parallel between the 1840's and the 1930's thus extends only to the monetary aspects of the economy. The declines in real national product and its components that occurred in the 1930's find only dim echoes in the deflation 90 years before. Investment may have fallen and parts of consumption stagnated, but the cataclysmic declines from previously sustained levels that characterized the 1930's were not apparent in the 1840's. There were many failures in the 1840's, and many parts of the economy suffered severe dislocations. But the failures related as much to the deflation as to the fall in investment, and the dislocations were limited to specific parts of the economy. Farmers, textile workers, and others found their money wages reduced. They were not unemployed, however, and their real incomes may not have fallen.[26]

As with the inflation, however, an account of the supply and demand for domestic goods does not tell the whole story. The supply and demand for imports have to be equilibrated as well as the supply and demand for domestic goods, and the two processes are not independent. In particular, the cessation of the British export of capital to the United States meant that the supply of British goods available to Americans had fallen. In the 1830's, Americans could buy more abroad than they sold; in the 1840's, they could not. At the prices and income levels of the 1830's, therefore, the demand for imports would have been greater than the supply. Had real income fallen in the early 1840's, this would have reduced the demand for imports, but real income did not fall. On the other hand, prices did fall, and imports became more expensive relative to domestic goods as a result. Americans were no longer eager to buy imported goods, and the supply and demand for imports was brought into balance.

Given that capital imports had ceased and real income had not fallen, prices in the United States had to fall to equilibrate

---

39, 264–66; Stanley Engerman and Robert W. Fogel, Data presented to the Purdue Conference, February, 1965.

26. See Smith, pp. 35–36, for a similar view.

the supply and demand for imports. If banks and the American public had not decided to hold more specie, specie would have been exported, and the money supply would have fallen anyway.[27] But it is not quite accurate to say that the cessation of capital imports was the cause of the deflation, and that the mechanism by which the supply of money fell was irrelevant. For capital imports stopped at least partly because the American states defaulted on their interest payments, and these states defaulted partly because the financial system of the United States was prostrated by the deflation. To some extent, therefore, the decline in British investment in the United States was a result of the crisis in the United States: It was a way in which the supply of British goods was decreased in response to the falling American demand.

The Role of Government

The Federal Government was an interested party in these fluctuations. Van Buren called a "panic session" of Congress in September, 1837, to deal with the crisis of that year, and efforts to alleviate the distress continued through the early 1840's.

Van Buren's program was composed of two parts: Relief from the immediate pressure and fidelity to the Jacksonian program. Relief was sought by many paths. Van Buren proposed that the fourth installment of the distribution scheduled for October 1, 1837 be postponed, that payment of duty bonds already posted by merchants be deferred, and that the government be authorized to issue Treasury notes to cover the deficit arising from the fall in tariff revenues. Fidelity to Jackson was to be demonstrated by the continuance of the Specie Circular and the withdrawal of all federal deposits from banks.

The measures for relief were enacted quickly by Congress. The Jacksonian acts fared less well. The Specie Circular was

27. At 1839 prices, more imports would have been bought than exports could pay for; foreign exchange would have risen to a premium; and specie would have been exported when the exchange rate reached a premium greater than the cost of shipping specie. See Chapter 3.

repealed in the regular session of Congress in 1838, and the proposal to keep the Treasury independent of banks languished until after the crisis of 1839. It was passed in the summer of 1840 and repealed a year later after the defeat of Van Buren in the election of 1840.[28]

The Specie Circular was still an important political issue in the fall of 1837, but its economic significance was even smaller then than a year earlier. The land boom had ended decisively around the end of 1836, and land sales had dropped by more than 70 percent from 1836 to 1837. They revived somewhat in 1839 from the low level of 1838, but they did not exceed the level of 1837 sales for many years.[29] The meagerness of the revival in 1839 shows the extent to which expectations changed in the years after 1836. The defeat of an Administration policy by Congress was not enough to revive the sanguine expectations of the mid-1830's.

Similarly, the proposal for an Independent Treasury, as the attempt to isolate the Treasury from the banking system was called, was of little economic importance in the late 1830's. The Federal Government, having seen the value of its bank deposits decline precipitously in the weeks following May 10, 1837, wanted to keep its monetary assets in the form of specie alone. The Federal Government was acting in concert with other members of the economy, and the net effect of the widespread desire to trade bank deposits and notes for specie was to raise the proportion of money held as specie from 13 percent in late 1836 to 35 percent in late 1842.[30]

This change drained specie from the banks where it could be used as reserves for bank notes and deposits. It decreased the supply of money in the United States and accentuated the deflation. Nevertheless, the Federal Government's part in this process was small. The government held only about 2 percent of the

28. Van Deusen, pp. 121–28, 155.
29. Table 4.3.
30. Tables 3.3, 5.2.

money supply, and the rise in the proportion of money held in specie was far too large to have been caused by a change in this part of the money supply alone.[31]

The Independent Treasury was re-enacted in 1846 after the deflation of the early 1840's had ended and shortly before the great gold discoveries in California. The deflationary effect of the government's desire for specie was more than offset in the 1850's by the continued infusion of California gold into the economy, and the effect of the Independent Treasury on the level of aggregate economic activity remained small.

The effects of the Independent Treasury would have been small in the early 1840's even if it had not been abolished in 1841, because the Federal Government was running a deficit and it could not accumulate a large cash reserve. The relevant data are shown in Table 5.3. The Federal Government had a surplus throughout the 1820's which continued throughout the boom of the 1830's. In 1837, however, both land sales and imports declined precipitously. The Federal Government's revenues, derived almost equally from land sales and customs duties in 1836, fell also. Revenue from land sales stayed low for many years thereafter. Tariff receipts rose briefly in 1839 in response to the renewed capital imports and the resultant import surplus of that year, but they otherwise stayed low until after the passage of a new, higher tariff in 1842.

The Federal Government's expenditures, on the other hand, did not decline in 1837. Considering the movements of prices, they really did not fall until 1839, and except for that year, they did not fall as much as revenues. The Federal Government's expenditures were primarily for the Army, the Navy, and pensions to soldiers of earlier wars. These expenses were not very responsive to cyclical changes in business conditions.

The change from surpluses during the boom before 1837 to deficits in the following deflation was sound fiscal policy, al-

31. Taus, p. 268. This estimate does not include the funds "on deposit" with the states as part of the Treasury's holdings.

TABLE 5.3

Federal Government Finances, 1830–44 †
(millions of dollars)

| | Revenue | | | | |
| | PUBLIC | | | | SURPLUS OR |
	CUSTOMS	LANDS	OTHER	EXPENDITURES	DEFICIT (—)
1830	21.9	2.3	.6	15.1	9.7
1831	24.2	3.2	1.1	15.2	13.3
1832	28.5	2.6	.8	17.3	14.6
1833	29.0	4.0	.9	23.0	10.9
1834	16.2	4.9	.7	18.6	3.2
1835	19.4	14.8	1.3	17.6	17.9
1836	23.4	24.9	2.5	30.9	20.0
1837	11.2	6.8	7.0	37.2	—12.3
1838	16.2	3.1	7.1	33.9	—7.6
1839	23.1	7.1	1.3	26.9	4.6
1840	13.5	3.3	2.7	24.3	—4.8
1841	14.5	1.4	1.0	26.5	—9.7
1842	18.2	1.3	.5	25.2	—5.2
1843 *	7.0	.9	.4	11.9	—3.6
1844	26.2	2.1	1.1	22.3	7.0

† Year ending December 31 through 1842, then June 30.
* Half-year only.
SOURCE: *U. S. Historical Statistics,* pp. 711–12. The surplus (deficit) may not exactly equal revenues minus expenditures due to rounding errors.

though it made the people of the time uneasy. During the boom, when there was an excess of demand, the Federal Government had been absorbing purchasing power from the economy. During the deflation, the government was injecting more into the economy than it was taking out, offsetting to some degree the deflationary trend.

The government's fiscal policy thus acted to reduce the fluctuations of the economy. In this it differed from the effects of the projected Independent Treasury. Like the Independent Treasury, however, it made little difference to the economy. The national product was approximately one and one-half billion dollars in these years; a deficit of $10 million was therefore less than 1 percent of the national product. In addition, much of the government's revenue came from the tariff, and fluctuations in this revenue were variations partly in taxes on foreigners. Without knowing how prices responded to the tariff—that is, without knowing the incidence of the tariff—it is impossible to say what part of the government's revenue was raised from the American people. To the extent that the deficit was due to a decline in taxes paid by foreigners, of course, it made no difference to the level of aggregate demand in the United States.

One year stands as an exception to this pattern. The change from a surplus of about $20 million in 1836 to a deficit of over $12 million in 1837 was definitely expansionary. As we noted in Chapter 4, the decline in land sales freed purchasing power for other uses, increasing the demand for goods and services. This decline shows up here as a rise in the government's deficit, acting to alleviate the effects of the Panic of 1837.

The government financed its deficits by issuing Treasury notes, which were securities with a maturity of only a year or two. It issued short-term securities rather than the more usual long-term bonds because it would have had difficulty selling the bonds for the price it wanted. The government assured the sale of the notes by giving to them some of the functions of money, notably the ability to be used in payments to the government. The notes therefore functioned partly as money, offsetting the general decline in the money supply. But although large numbers of notes were issued, they came due and were redeemed rapidly. The volume of notes outstanding at any one time consequently was never very large. It never amounted to even 1 percent of the money supply.[32]

The Federal Government moved to reduce its deficit in 1842 by raising the tariff. From the standpoint of modern fiscal policy, this was the exact wrong thing to do, although it was not

32. See the discussion of Treasury notes in the Appendix.

likely to have any more effect on the economy than the deficits had had. And to the extent that the people of the time thought that it was a proper way to cure a depression and became more willing to spend as a result, it was a good thing. In any case, the recovery began at about the same time as the new tariff took effect, and commentators—then and now—have seen this as a causal relation.[33]

The states had taken the opposite route to fiscal balance, reducing their expenditures in the early 1840's in response to falling revenues. Like the Federal Government's efforts to eliminate its deficit, these reductions reduced demand and accentuated the deflation. Like the federal actions also, they were too small to have an important effect. The declines in state expenditures were on the order of magnitude of 1 percent of income, and since they were generally balanced by a decline in revenue, their influence was muted.[34]

The role of government in the deflation, then, was minimal. Following 19th-century orthodoxy, the various levels of government attempted to bring their expenditures and receipts into balance. The states reduced their expenditures when their receipts fell; the Federal Government endured deficits for several years and then moved to raise its revenues. These actions acted to depress demand at a time of low demand. They consequently impeded recovery, although they were too small to impede it much, and the Federal Government's tardiness in raising its revenues produced deficits that acted in the opposite direction. Reforms that were undertaken or attempted in these years, like the Independent Treasury and a national bankruptcy law, had little effect on the deflation. As with the Second Bank, the po-

33. The evidence for this view is restricted to the coincidence of tariff and recovery just noted; it is by no means conclusive. See Temin, 1964, pp. 23–24.
34. The Middle Atlantic region is an exception to this generalization. A large deficit about 1840 was transformed into a surplus in the succeeding few years. The connection of this deficit with the failure of the Bank of the United States (a Pennsylvania bank after 1836) is unclear. Davis and Legler, pp. 532–33.

litical significance of the government's actions in the early 1840's outweighed their economic effects.

What happened in the early 1840's was roughly the opposite of what had happened in the 1830's. In the earlier decade, the supply of money had risen as a result of causes arising largely outside the American economy. This produced a construction boom, but because production could not rise as much as prices, the effect was primarily to raise prices. In the 1840's, the falling supply of money led to falling prices, and prices fell far enough to obviate a need for production to fall in addition. Business was deranged during the price fall, but the panics were short-lived. The growth of income was below its usual rate, but there was no decline in income comparable to the depression of the 1930's. In the 1830's and 1840's, prices were far more flexible than production—in both directions.

6

Conclusions

~~~~~~

WE OPENED THIS INQUIRY with a summary of the traditional story of the Jacksonian boom and its aftermath; we close with a summary of the replacement offered here and some comments about its implications.

To start, the political importance of Jackson's "destruction" of the Second Bank of the United States far outweighed the economic. The unsupported bank expansion that the Bank War has been thought to have initiated simply did not take place. Banks did not expand credit without cause, and they do not seem to have regarded government deposits as additions to reserves. They kept more or less constant reserve ratios throughout the boom—excepting 1834, of course—and the supply of money expanded for reasons unconnected with the Bank War.

Unfortunately for Jackson's reputation, the Bank War coincided with two developments, one in England and one in China, that together produced inflation. A series of unusually good harvests in England initiated a boom in that country about 1832, and British eagerness to invest in the United States and to buy American cotton rose and stayed high for several years. For the British to export capital to the United States, the United States had to buy more in Britain than it sold—that is, to run a trade deficit. And in order for the American demand for British goods to rise, prices in the United States had to rise to make imported goods cheaper, and therefore preferable, to domestically produced ones.[1] The British demand for cotton caused

1. Demand for imports can also rise because national income rises, but the national income in the United States could not rise enough to

prices in America to rise higher than they otherwise would have done; American exports were increasing at the same time as American imports, and a trade deficit was harder to produce.

For prices in America to rise, the supply of money in America had to rise. Since banks were not willing to expand without increased reserves, new reserves—that is, specie—were needed to let the quantity of money rise. This specie could not have come from Britain because the Bank of England was not willing to let its reserves slip across the Atlantic. The Old Lady of Threadneedle Street showed as much by her actions in 1836 and 1837; she would have acted sooner if need had arisen. Consequently, the English boom by itself could not have caused the American inflation.

Coincidentally, however, changes were taking place in the Far East that had important ramifications for this process. The Chinese were buying opium in increasing quantities, and they no longer desired silver to hoard. They wanted silver to exchange for opium, and any silver the United States sent to them would have been sent to England in payment for Indian opium. This transshipment was avoided by substituting American credit for Mexican silver, and the United States retained the silver imports from Mexico that it had sent to the Orient in earlier years. This silver went into bank reserves in America, allowing prices to rise and the demand for imports to increase. It may be said that the Chinese enabled the British to export capital to the United States by releasing silver to be used as a base for American monetary expansion, or that the capital flow from Britain to the United States allowed the Americans to keep their silver instead of sending it to the East.

The high British demand for cotton acted to increase the inflation by reducing the American trade deficit, but it also acted to retard the inflation by setting off a land boom. As the price of cotton soared upward, speculative fever kept pace.

---

produce the desired import surplus. There was substantially full employment at the start of the boom, and there were no technological changes that markedly increased the productivity of labor.

Land sales of the Federal Government rose dramatically in 1835 and 1836, and part of the increase in the money supply went into land purchases. The Federal Government accumulated a surplus, and these funds were removed from circulation. It was thought at the time that these funds were used as the basis for further monetary expansion, but we have shown that this did not happen. The government continued to sell land at a constant price, and funds that otherwise would have been used to raise prices rested in the government's surplus. We have no way of knowing whether the net effect of the cotton price's two offsetting influences was positive or negative.

The inflation had to end, and even be replaced by deflation, if the British stopped exporting capital to the United States. The Bank of England thought it was losing specie to the United States in late 1836 and acted to restrain the capital flow. This produced a commercial crisis in the United States, but the breaking point did not come until the price of cotton fell in early 1837. As this important price fell, the credit structure built with cotton as security collapsed. Banks in the United States refused to preserve the convertibility of their notes and deposits into specie and thus into foreign exchange at a fixed rate; the United States effectively devalued for a short time.

Andrew Jackson has been blamed for the Panic of 1837, but it is clear that he was not the villain. The accumulating surplus had created a political problem, and the distribution of the surplus to the states offered a solution. The distribution would have created some hardship for the banking system, but it was not qualitatively different from previous governmental transactions, and it would not have produced a crisis. The Specie Circular, issued to offset the inflationary effects of the distribution, similarly was not a cause of the panic. The boom had been caused by a tenuous balance of independent forces; when this balance was lost, one or the other of the forces was bound to cause trouble. As it turned out, a diminution in the capital flow from England to America was the force that led to the crisis.

The effects of the panic were mild, however, and the economy soon recovered from them. The British continued to lend to the United States once the Bank of England had accumulated a satisfactory volume of reserves, the price of cotton revived in early 1839 due to a short harvest and to the effects of Nicholas Biddle's speculations, and the funds distributed to the states were spent by them on a variety of projects. The first and second of these developments restored the financial system to its pre-panic health and allowed American banks to resume specie payments. The restored financial system cooperated with the demand from the states to produce renewed prosperity in 1839.

This prosperity did not last long. A bad wheat harvest in England in 1838 caused the British to export specie in return for imports of wheat in 1839, and the Bank of England tightened credit once again to replenish its reserves. A bumper crop of cotton in 1839 caused the price of cotton to fall in early 1840, and many banks followed the precedent of 1837 by suspending payments. The panic was not as severe in 1839 as it had been in 1837, but it marked the end of the boom.

States ceased their expenditures and defaulted on their bonds. The British replied by ceasing to export capital to the United States. Simultaneously, banks increased their reserve ratios, and people raised the proportion of their funds they wanted to hold in coin. The cessation of British lending meant the end of the opportunity for the United States to finance a trade deficit. The rise in the two monetary ratios lowered the supply of money, reducing the demand for both American and imported goods. The falling demand for American goods produced falling prices; the falling demand for imports ended the trade deficit. The effects of the panic thus produced deflation in two ways: Through its effect on the balance of trade and by its effect on the supply of money. As with the inflation, it is not possible to say that the international capital movements or the change in the quantity of money alone produced the deflation; they acted together, and their results are inseparable.

The deflation was as dramatic as the preceding inflation,

and its effect on national income appears to have been as small. Many businesses failed, but the resultant change in ownership did not interrupt production. Agricultural production was unaffected by the deflation, and the growing industrial sector of the economy continued to expand. Only the part of the economy servicing trade and commerce suffered, and the overall effects of the decline in trade were small. There is no evidence of widespread unemployment or of distress not produced by the price fall alone during the early 1840's.

Inflation, crisis, deflation: This was the story of the Jacksonian era. The sequence has been known for a long time, but the roles played by historical personnages have been confused. Contemporary observers blamed Andrew Jackson, and historians have agreed. Yet analysis shows that Jackson was not the prime mover in the inflation, the crises, or the deflation. His policies did not help the economy to adjust to the harsh requirements of external forces, but they were of little importance beside these far stronger influences.

Andrew Jackson, then, did not pay a high cost for his destruction of the Second Bank. He did not initiate a speculative mania, and he did not plunge the economy into crisis and depression. To the extent that these events have been blamed on his actions, he has been victimized by external events. It would not be appropriate here to defend Jackson's policies, but it must be insisted that they were not tested by the events of the 1830's. We cannot say what would have happened had Jackson not entered into his "war" with Biddle, but it is doubtful that the banking system would have reacted any differently to the shocks it received had the Bank of the United States continued as the government's fiscal agent.

The economy was not as unstable as historians have assumed; there do not appear to have been forces within the banking system leading inevitably toward a crisis unless restrained by superior force. The banking system did not have the ability to adapt to external shocks, but it did not produce sharp inflations like the one culminating in 1837 without external help. The antebellum economy was vulnerable to disturbing influences, but it was not a source of them. The distinction is important.

Finally, the economy possessed a structure of some analytic interest. It functioned to a large extent in the fashion described by what we now call classical economic theory. Prices were flexible, they could vary to facilitate capital transfers, and they could change radically without destroying the ability of the economy to operate near capacity. Yet the price-specie-flow mechanism did not operate according to the textbook rules; without a supply of silver from "outside the system," the mechanism would not have worked. And the price level, while variable, was not "neutral." It mattered what the price level was, or at least what the price of cotton was, because a large part of the antebellum financial system used cotton for security. When its price fell, the system broke down, and a decline in prices was considerably more difficult to effect than a rise.

As Gallatin said, Jackson "found the currency of the country in a sound and left it in a deplorable state," but most of the change was not of Jackson's doing. In destroying the Second Bank of the United States, he had closed off an area of possible future experimentation, but he had not precipitated a "bank-boom-bust sequence." The economic fluctuations of the Jacksonian era may still be deplored, but they cannot any longer be used as an argument against Jacksonianism.

Appendix on Data

~~~~~~

THIS APPENDIX describes the sources of the monetary data used in the text. We begin with a discussion of the data on banks. We then combine these data with data on specie movements and supplies to get estimates of the supply of money. Finally, we describe the sources for the data on the international flows of specie.

Congress passed a resolution in 1832 requesting the Secretary of the Treasury to compile data on the conditions of state banks and to report them to Congress once a year. The Secretary did so, starting with a report giving conditions as of January 1, 1834. These reports are the basis of all the aggregate monetary data cited for the later antebellum period.[1]

These data have certain problems. They were presented to Congress in the first week of January each year, and their claim to show conditions as of the first of January must be interpreted liberally. Obviously, the data refer to the end of the previous year, with the precise dating depending on the speed of communication as much as anything else. In addition, returns were estimated for 100 banks in 1834, and a declining number thereafter. The need to estimate the returns from large numbers of banks appears to have been connected with the problems of

---

1. The reports are summarized in U. S. Congress, House Document 111, 26th Congress, 2nd Session (1841), and House Document 68, 31st Congress, 1st Session (1850). Summary tables can be found on p. 1455 of House Document 111 and pp. 422–25 of House Document 68. These tables are reproduced in the *Reports* of the U. S. Comptroller of the Currency, for example, 1876, pp. XLIV-XLV, without the accompanying state data.

initiating the reports; by 1836 the number of estimated banks
had fallen to eight. These problems are not serious. The first
can be removed by redating the estimates, and the second is
relevant only for the first few years.[2]

These data can be used to construct bank balance sheets—
as was done in Table 2.1—or to compute the reserve ratios of
banks. We do the latter here as a first step toward an estimate of
the money supply.

We first compute the gross obligation of banks. These consisted of three items, only the first two of which represented
obligations to the public. The first liability consisted of bank
notes. As Gouge said in 1833, "Bank notes are *simple evi-
dences of debt* due by the Banks."[3] In other words, a bank
note was a promise by a bank to pay a certain amount of specie
on demand.

The second liability consisted of deposits owned by the public. There was considerable confusion about the precise nature
of deposits, but Gouge noted correctly that deposits and notes
were equivalent. His argument was simple: You can get notes
for checks.[4] Others have been confused by intricacies of bank
balance sheets. Each liability had an offsetting asset, and each
asset had an offsetting liability, for the asset and liability sides
of the balance sheet had to be equal. A deposit was created in
return either for a payment of specie to the bank or for a
promise by the depositor to pay the bank at a later date—that
is, for a loan. Specie and loans were bank assets; the offsetting
obligation to cash checks at the pleasure of the depositor was
clearly a liability. (A bank's original assets were offset by the
capital rather than liabilities, as people paid for their shares in

2. Schwartz went back to the original state reports for New York
and Pennsylvania and recomputed the aggregate data for these states.
Except for minor differences of definition, she reproduced the Secretary
of the Treasury's results. See Anna Jacobson Schwartz, "Pennsylvania
and New York Banking Statistics," unpublished paper for the National
Bureau of Economic Research.
3. Gouge, p. 54, his emphasis.
4. *Ibid.*, p. 23.

specie or took out loans to pay for them. This was recognized in the bank balance sheet by making assets equal the sum of liabilities and capital.)

There has been some discussion in the literature of the distinction between deposits of specie and deposits created by giving loans, the latter being referred to as credit or book credit to differentiate them from "true" deposits. The distinction may have been a legal one, but it is not an economic one. Consider the hypothetical case where a bank received $100 in specie, terming the obligation to return it to its owner a deposit. It then discounted a commercial bill for $50, paying out notes for the bill. Assume the notes were returned to the bank and redeemed for specie, the deposit meanwhile being untouched. The bank then had a deposit of $100 and only $50 in specie. The deposit had not been created in response to a loan, but events had transformed it into a deposit backed by a loan. It is clear that the clue to banking practice is not the distinction between various forms of liabilities, but instead the nature of the specie reserves held against these liabilities.[5]

Notes and deposits were owed by banks to individuals. The third liability of banks consisted of obligations between banks. Banks borrowed from each other and made deposits in other banks in the same way as individuals, and banks, consequently, had other banks as depositors. The deposit of another bank was as much an obligation as the deposit of an individual, and we must include it among bank liabilities. To avoid confusion, we follow contemporary practice in referring to a deposit made by banks simply as funds "due to other banks." The gross obligations of banks, therefore, consisted of bank notes, deposits and amounts due to other banks.[6]

5. Hammond has a clear discussion of the economic equivalence of all deposits (pp. 80–84) and of the terminological confusion about them (pp. 137–40). For examples of recent confusion, see Redlich and Christman, pp. 293–94; Baughman, pp. 433–35.

6. *U. S. Historical Statistics,* p. 625, presents the sum of deposits and amounts due other banks as "deposits." They, therefore, include interbank deposits with other deposits, and the total must be used with care.

These liabilities plus the capital were offset completely by assets, but some assets were internal to the banking system, and it is more appropriate in deriving an estimate of the money supply to subtract them from the liabilities than to add them to assets. Deposits held in other banks comprised one such asset. For every amount "due to other banks" shown on one bank's balance sheet, there was an equal amount "due from other banks" shown on some other bank's balance sheet. Any single bank could owe more or less to other banks than was owed by other banks to it, but for the banking system as a whole, the amounts had to be equal. By subtracting the amounts "due from other banks" from liabilities rather than adding it to assets, we avoid overstating the total obligations of the banking system to the public.[7]

Similarly, the notes of other banks received in the course of trade were assets to any single bank, but not to the banking system as a whole. The notes that any bank held can be subtracted from the total of its notes outstanding to get a figure representing net note liability. For the banking system as a whole, this procedure will subtract from the total amount of notes issued by banks those notes held by banks other than the issuing bank, leaving only notes held by the public. Net liabilities—that is, notes and deposits *plus* the amounts due to other banks *less* the amounts due from other banks and notes of other banks held—therefore represent an estimate of each bank's liabilities that can be summed to find the total liabilities of the banking system as a whole to the public.[8]

The reserve ratios of banks can be computed as the ratio of their reserves to their net liabilities. It will be noted that this

7. Macesich, 1960, assumed deposits included interbank deposits and subtracted the amount due from other banks from deposits without adding the amount due to other banks. Walker did not adjust for interbank obligations at all. See Amasa Walker, *The Science of Wealth* (Boston, 1866), p. 161.

8. Van Fenstermaker did not subtract these assets from liabilities in computing the reserve ratio, and the liabilities he computed for the banking system as a whole overstate the total liabilities of the banking system. See Van Fenstermaker, p. 68.

procedure includes interbank obligations in the calculation of the reserve ratio of a particular bank, state, or region, but that these interbank obligations cancel out in the calculation of the reserve ratio of the banking system as a whole. Reserves, of course, were simply the specie held in banks.[9]

In Table A.1 we compare the reserve ratio for all state banks calculated in this fashion from the reports of the Secretary of Treasury with an alternate estimate of the reserve ratio for state banks calculated from Van Fenstermaker's data. Van Fenstermaker went back to the original state reports and compiled banking data for the years before the Treasury did so. He continued his estimates through 1837, and the two sets of estimates are presented in Table A.1 for the years in which they overlap.

The correspondence is reasonably good for 1833 (which the Treasury reported as January, 1834). Both sets of estimates have data for about 80 percent of the state banks, and the differences between them probably come from differences in their samples. The two sets of estimates agree very well for the next two years, but for 1836 and 1837 Van Fenstermaker's estimates of reserves and liabilities are larger than the Treasury's by an appreciable margin. Both sets of data show the same reserve ratios, and we may have confidence in these ratios, but the difference in scale shown in the two sources is mysterious.

There was no good way to reconcile the differences between these estimates, and we have had to acknowledge the existence of both. This has been done explicitly in Tables 3.4 and 4.2, where the data from both sources have been shown. (Data for 1833 were not reported in these tables due to the difficulty of

9. "Specie funds" often have been counted as part of reserves, but this is not valid. Specie funds were highly liquid assets that could be converted easily into specie by any individual bank. But while any individual bank might be able to get specie by, say, redeeming a note of the Bank of the United States, the banking system as a whole could not. These items were not true reserves, and they have not been entered as reserves here. In addition, they were never more than 10 percent of the value of specie held in banks except in 1834 when a clerical error included all specie in with specie funds.

TABLE A.1

Data on State Banks From Two Sources, 1833–37

END OF YEAR	Reserves [a]		Net Obligations [b]		Reserve Ratio	
	TREASURY	VAN FENSTER-MAKER	TREASURY	VAN FENSTER-MAKER	TREASURY	VAN FENSTER-MAKER
	($ millions)		($ millions)		(percent)	
1833	14	17	122	127	11	13
1834	28	28	139	143	20	19
1835	32	33	196	197	16	17
1836	38	44	241	270	16	16
1837	35	39	179	202	20	19

SOURCES: *House Document 111, pp. 1418, 1455; Van Fenstermaker, pp. 66–68. The Treasury data were obtained by subtracting the data for the Bank of the United States from the total for all banks before 1836 and redating the estimates; Van Fenstermaker's data were expanded to allow for his partial sample by dividing his totals by the proportion of banks reported.*
[a] Specie. Treasury specie was taken to be nine tenths of specie funds in 1833 as no specie was reported, and this proportion held in other years. The difference in reporting did not come from a difference in the state bank reports. House Document 111, pp. 1419–55.
[b] Notes in circulation and deposits plus amounts due other banks less notes of other banks held and amounts due from other banks.

disaggregating the chaotic first-year reports of the Treasury.) The two sources have been spliced for the estimates of the money supply. Van Fenstermaker's data have been used for the years through 1833.[10] The Treasury data have been used for the later years. As these data continue beyond 1837, the scale given by them for 1836 and 1837 was used in place of the scale shown by Van Fenstermaker. A different procedure would not have affected our arguments about the reserve ratios of banks.

These data can be combined with data on the Bank of the United States and on specie outside banks to provide the raw

10. In all years, his totals have been divided by the proportion of chartered banks reporting to get an estimate for all banks. This assumes his sample was representative of the other banks.

materials for an estimate of the quantity of money. Data on the Second Bank are readily available.[11] Data on specie outside banks, on the other hand, are problematical.

The data on the total specie in the country come from the 1896 *Report* of the Comptroller of the Currency, where they are given without citation. We cannot trace them back to their source as a result, and we must assess their reliability in other ways. We compare the Comptroller's series with a constructed series of our own and with contemporary comments.

A new series for the specie in the United States was constructed by starting with the Comptroller's estimate for late 1829 (which he labeled January, 1830) and computing changes from it. Changes could come from two sources, domestic mining and foreign trade. Domestic mining did not add more than one million dollars to the specie in the country in any single year before 1848, but it was extremely important thereafter. Exports and imports of specie were important at all times.

This constructed series is compared with the Comptroller's series in Table A.2. The similarity between the two series from 1829 through 1842 or 1843 is clear. The constructed series does

11. House Document 111, p. 1418, or for more detail, U. S. Congress, Senate Document 128, 25th Congress, 2nd Session (1838), pp. 208–11. Van Fenstermaker gave totals for the Bank of the United States, but he made a conceptual error in their derivation. The Bank listed the notes issued by each branch, and Van Fenstermaker used this total to get the circulation of the Bank's notes by office of issue. However, the Bank held a large inventory of its own notes, and the volume of its notes in circulation was only about half of the volume of notes issued. As the location of this inventory was not given, the circulation of the Bank by region is hard to measure. Nevertheless, Van Fenstermaker's use of the volume of notes issued greatly overstated the Bank's outstanding liabilities. For example, Van Fenstermaker's 1834 data and the Treasury's 1835 data are taken from the same source: Senate Document 128, pp. 2–6. (Van Fenstermaker used only pp. 2–5. See his pp. 238–47.) The original source shows that the Bank of the United States had issued notes worth $38.8 million, but that $17.3 million were on hand and $4.1 million were in transit between branches of the Bank. Only $17.3 million were in the hands of the public. Van Fenstermaker's data show a circulation equal to $33.1 million. This is not precisely equal to any of the Treasury totals, but it is approximately twice as large as the correct figure.

not provide a check on the level of the Comptroller's series because it starts at the same point, but it does provide a check on the rate of change. The rise in the amount of specie that is such an important part of the story told here is apparent to both series. There are differences between the two series in particular years, but the overall change from 1829 to 1837 is almost the same.

Some of the differences in individual years result from a

TABLE A.2

Specie in the United States and in Banks, 1820–58
(millions of dollars)

Specie in the U.S.

END OF YEAR	COMPTROLLER OF THE CURRENCY	CONSTRUCTED	SPECIE IN BANKS
1820		41	21
1821		39	24
1822		32	13
1823		31	18
1824		32	21
1825		29	18
1826		32	19
1827		32	18
1828		31	18
1829	33	33	20
1830	32	39	24
1831	30	37	22
1832	31	38	23
1833	41	43	27
1834	51	59	44
1835	65	67	40
1836	73	77	38
1837	88	81	35
1838	87	96	45
1839	83	93	33

Specie in the U.S.

END OF YEAR	COMPTROLLER OF THE CURRENCY	CONSTRUCTED	SPECIE IN BANKS
1840	80	94	35
1841	80	90	28
1842	90	90	34
1843	100	112	50
1844	96	113	44
1845	97	110	42
1846	120	111	35
1847	112	135	46
1848	120	135	44
1849	154	177	45
1850	186	225	49
1851	204	258	N.A.
1852	236	281	47
1853	241	326	59
1854	250	355	54
1855	250	359	59
1856	260	374	58
1857	260	375	74
1858	250	374	105

SOURCES: *Same Sources as Table A.1, plus U.S. Comptroller of the Currency, Report, 1896, I, 544; U. S. Historical Statistics, pp. 371, 538. The constructed series was set equal to the Comptroller's series for 1829.*

difference of timing. The Comptroller's series shows the specie in the United States at the close of the calendar year, while the constructed series shows it at the close of the fiscal year. The three-month discrepancy may explain why the constructed series continues to rise for one year after the Comptroller's series had reached its peak in 1837, or why the sharp rise shown in the constructed series in 1834 is paralleled by a more regular rise in the Comptroller's series. It cannot account for the difference between the two series in 1830, and we do not know the source of this discrepancy.

Further evidence of the similarity between the two series is provided by statistical means. The two estimates of the specie in the United States are highly correlated in the years 1829–43; the correlation coefficient between them is .98. Despite the differences between them, the constructed series "predicts" the movements of the Comptroller's series with a very high degree of accuracy. There is little doubt that the rise in the supply of specie during the 1830's is very well documented.[12]

The amount of specie in the United States at any one time —as opposed to the change in this amount—is less easy to document. As noted in Chapter 3, the argument is not changed very much if the total amount of specie was larger than the estimates, provided the change has been accurately reported. It is foolish to ask if the estimates are too low, for they could not be much lower. Data on specie in banks are also presented in Table A.2, and it is apparent that the estimates of specie outside banks are very low in some years. According to the Comptroller of the Currency and the Secretary of the Treasury, there was only about seven or eight million dollars of specie outside banks in the first half of the 1830's. This is a very small amount, and reduction of the estimates of specie in the United States would run the risk of making it negative.

But is this very small amount reasonable? Was the United States almost exclusively using paper money at that time? Informed contemporaries certainly thought so. Gouge said in 1833 that "the sprinkling of silver [in the United States] has only the effect of keeping up the reputation of the paper." Secretary of the Treasury Taney said in an April, 1834, report that the amount of specie outside banks was only four million dollars. He explained this figure as follows: "In some of the States the circulation of bank notes below five dollars is prohibited by

12. It is easy to construct an alternate set of money-supply estimates from the constructed data on specie. The constructed estimates will be even more highly correlated with the estimates of the money supply shown in Tables 3.3 and 5.2 than the two specie series are with each other because the banking data will be the same in both estimates.

law, and in these states there is a considerable amount of specie passing from hand to hand, and forming part of the ordinary circulating medium." The implication is that little or no specie circulated in the other states. Secretary of the Treasury Woodbury said in his December, 1835 report that the amount of specie in the United States was greater than $64 million. (The Comptroller's estimate for that date is $65 million.) He said a year later that the specie outside banks in 1833 was about $4 million, probably with Taney's estimate in mind, and he estimated that the specie outside banks had grown rapidly to $28 million in December, 1836. (The Comptroller's estimate shows $35 million at that time.) The estimates in Table A.2 are in firm agreement with the views of informed contemporaries.[13]

The two estimates of the quantity of specie in the United States diverge in the mid-1840's, and the constructed series rises faster than the Comptroller's after that. It is possible that the Comptroller's series underestimated the volume of domestic mining activity and the amount of specie in the country as a result. If so, the estimate of the money supply shown in Table 5.2 is too low, as is the proportion of money held by the public as specie. In this case, the popular reaction from the "paper-money inflation" of the 1830's was stronger than is implied in Table 5.2, but little else is changed.

We are now ready to construct an estimate of the money supply. The conventional definition of money is the sum of bank deposits and currency outside banks, where currency in this context means the sum of specie and bank notes. Money, in other words, consists of those items held by the public that serve as a medium of exchange.[14]

We follow this definition here and define money to be equal to the net liabilities of banks—that is, bank notes and deposits —plus specie in the hands of the public—that is, not in banks.

13. Gouge, p. 57; U.S. Treasury, *Reports of the Secretary,* III, 451, 649, 695, 696.
14. Contemporaries often used a different definition of money: "Bank notes are promises to pay on demand a given quantity of coin; they are promises to pay *money,* but they are not *money* in themselves."

The results are shown in Tables 3.3 and 5.2. Other definitions of money are possible, but the differences between the estimates in Tables 3.3 and 5.2 and those shown elsewhere derive more from confusion about the data than differences of definition.[15]

There are several characteristics of our estimates that are of special interest. First, the Federal Government—as well as state governments—was considered to be a member of the public. This is contrary to 20th-century practice, but the role of the government was different then than now. The government now has the power to create money. Consequently, the amount of money it holds is of little interest. In the antebellum period, the government could not create money (except by the means to be discussed shortly), and it had to make the same choices as individuals about where and how to hold its money. It held it in banks before 1840 and under the mattress—that is, in the Independent Treasury—for most years between 1840 and the Civil War.

Including the Federal Government with the public has two advantages. It enables us to treat the government's monetary holdings as part of the total in the discussion of the expansion

---

Appleton, p. 6, his emphasis. Money to Appleton was simply specie. It seems more useful to consider all those things that were readily interchangeable with specie at a fixed price as money also.

15. Several confusions have already been noted. For another ex-example, consider the data in *U. S. Historical Statistics,* p. 647. A series is reported there for currency in circulation as of June 30. This appears to be an independent series because the Secretary of the Treasury's data were dated January 1. The data were taken from the 1896 *Report* of the Comptroller of the Currency, Vol. I, p. 544. The Comptroller added together the volume of bank notes issued and the amount of specie in the United States to get what he called "total money in the United States." The compilers of *Historical Statistics* corrected this appellation to read, "total currency in the United States," but we must remember that the data include bank notes held by banks as well as bank notes in circulation. The data on bank notes came from the Secretary of the Treasury; it is not known where the confusion in dating originated. The series on the amount of specie is the one we have been discussing here. (*Historical Statistics* also has data on currency in the Treasury; this is the series the Comptroller reported as *specie* in the Treasury.) Any data dated June 30 come from this source.

of the 1830's, and it enables us to treat the federal and state governments symmetrically. There is no way to identify the holdings of state governments, and the logic of giving special treatment to the Federal Government and not the state governments is obscure.[16]

Second, all bank notes were valued at par. Bank notes circulated at discounts that varied extensively over time and place, but this is not reflected in our estimates. The value of the quantity of money at any specific place was then actually smaller than shown in Tables 3.3 and 5.2, because the notes from distant banks were worth less than their full value. This problem is more serious for the earlier than the later years, because the discounts on bank notes were falling over time.

Similarly, the estimates were not adjusted for the discounts on bank notes and deposits during the suspensions of specie payments. As a result, the estimates are too high for 1837 and 1839–42. Table 4.1 shows that the discount on bank notes and deposits in New York was about 5 percent at the end of 1837; the error in our estimate for 1837, consequently, is less than that. The discount in Cincinnati ranged generally between 5 and 10 percent from early 1840 to early 1842.[17]

In addition, we did not include in the estimate of money a variety of special obligations issued in the years after 1837. The Bank of the United States, operating under its Pennsylvania charter, issued "post-notes" in an attempt to acquire liquid assets. These notes were not redeemable in specie until some time after they were issued (hence their name); and they were,

16. It is not clear that we have sufficient data to identify the deposits of the Federal Government. Taus, pp. 267–70, reported a series which came from the *Annual Report of the Secretary of the Treasury,* 1918, pp. 620–22, where it is given without sources. This series shows the government's balances to have been entirely in the form of bank deposits through 1835 (except for two years before 1830). It therefore conflicts with the series in the 1896 *Report* of the Comptroller of the Currency, I, 544, which shows the government's balances to have been entirely in specie through 1835. See also Elliot, 1845, p. 1019, for data on Treasury balances.

17. Berry, pp. 590–91.

therefore, a type of short-term security. They were roughly the equivalent of commercial bills, but they may have circulated like ordinary bank notes, in which case they formed part of the money supply.[18] The Federal Government was also pressed for cash in these years, and it borrowed money by issuing notes— that is, short-term securities. These notes had characteristics both of short-term debt and of money, and they could be used to pay taxes or duties. To the extent they functioned as money, they should be counted in our estimate.

The Bank of the Untied States had post-notes outstanding from late 1837, until its failure at the start of 1841. The Federal Government had notes outstanding from 1837 through 1877, but almost all the notes had been redeemed by 1844. The sum of these two types of notes reached its peak at the end of 1838, when it totaled something under $19 million, or less than 10 percent of the money supply. If this sum were added to the money supply, it would show the rise in the money supply in 1838 to have been higher than that shown in Table 3.3. The Second Bank failed in 1841, and the volume of Treasury notes outstanding fell rapidly in the early 1840's. Nevertheless, inclusion of them in the money supply would reduce the fall in the money supply shown after 1838. It should be remembered, however, that a correct valuation of the depreciated bank notes in these years would work in the opposite direction.[19]

Finally, it must be noted that the data for the 1820's are considerably less secure than the data for subsequent years. The data for the 1820's were derived from a sample including only one half to two thirds of all banks. To the extent that these

18. See Smith, Chapter 11, and Hammond, 504–06, for the Bank's use of post-notes.

19. For data on the Second Bank, see House Document 111, p. 1418. For data on the Treasury notes, see Rafael A. Bayley, "The National Loans of the United States from July 4, 1776 to June 30, 1880," in *U. S. Census,* Tenth, VII (Washington, 1881), pp. 178–79. The Bank had roughly $8 million "other liabilities," which included post–notes, outstanding from late 1837 on. The government had the following amounts of notes outstanding at the end of each year starting with 1837, and ending with 1843 (in millions): $3, $10, $3, $5, $8, $11, $3.

banks were not representative of their fellows, the estimates are in error. The estimates for later years are based on more inclusive surveys and have fewer errors from this source.[20]

The estimates of the quantity of money in Tables 3.3 and 5.2 thus embody the best data available. Despite the apparent diversity of estimates available for the antebellum money supply, we have seen that they all derive from the same sources. These sources are subject to error, but the obvious ones are either not large or not quantifiable. Until more data are found, the estimates presented here appear to be the best that can be made.

Having shown how the estimates of the money supply were derived, we turn now to the data on specie flows, the principal factor causing the supply of money to rise in the 1830's. The data in Table 3.5 show the imports of specie into the United States by country of origin. The value of net imports does not equal the change in the value of specie in the United States reported in Tables 3.3 and 5.2 because of the difference between the two series for the value of specie reported in Table A.2. In addition, however, the net imports shown in Table 3.5 differ from changes in the constructed series for specie in the United States for two reasons. First, the constructed series in Table A.2 includes the output of domestic mines as well as gains from international trade. And second, the export data in Table 3.5 do not include the domestic exports of gold and silver which are included in the data reported in *U. S. Historical Statistics* and used in Table A.2. These exports were omitted because they were labeled "manufactures of gold and silver coin" for the years 1831–37. Manufactures of gold and silver were commodity exports, and although they used monetary gold and silver as raw materials, the raw materials were worth far less than the manufactures made of them. Inclusion of these items would, therefore, distort the picture shown in Table 3.5, although the total amount of them in 1831–37 was only $7 million, and their impact on the total picture shown in Table

20. Van Fenstermaker, p. 68. The estimates of specie in the U. S. for the 1820's were taken from the constructed series in Table A.2.

A.2 was minimal. (They went almost entirely to England, France, and Canada.)

The sources for the data in Table 3.5 are the annual *Reports on Commerce and Navigation* compiled by the U.S. Treasury Department. They were reported to Congress and can be most easily found in the congressional documents. Table A.3 gives the actual citations.

TABLE A.3

Sources for Table 3.5

FISCAL YEAR	CONGRESS	SESSION	HOUSE DOCUMENT
1825	19	1	148
1826	19	2	120
1827	20	1	253
1828	20	2	137
1829	21	1	49
1830	21	2	140
1831	22	1	230
1832	22	2	109
1833	23	1	355
1834	23	2	187
1835	24	1	258
1836	24	2	188
1837	25	2	372
1838	25	3	253
1839	26	1	251

NOTE: These House Documents are the annual *Reports on Commerce and Navigation.*

References Cited

Appleton, Nathan, *Remarks on Currency and Banking* (Boston, 1841).

Baughman, James P., "Early American Checks: Forms and Functions," *Business History Review*, XLI (Winter, 1967), 421–35.

Bayley, Rafael, A., "The National Loans of the United States from July 4, 1776, to June 30, 1880," in *U. S. Census*, Tenth, VII (Washington, 1881).

Benson, Lee, *The Concept of Jacksonian Democracy* (Princeton: Princeton University Press, 1961).

Benton, Thomas Hart, *Thirty Years' View*. 2 vols. (New York, 1854).

Berry, Thomas Senior, *Western Prices Before 1861* (Cambridge: Harvard University Press, 1943).

Biddle, Nicholas, Letter to J. Q. Adams, Nov. 11, 1836. Reprinted in *Niles' Weekly Register*, LI (Dec. 17, 1836), 243–45.

Biddle, Nicholas, *Correspondence*. R. C. McGrane, ed. (Boston: Houghton Mifflin, 1919).

Bourne, Edward G., *History of the Surplus Revenue of 1837* (New York, 1885).

Buck, Norman S., *The Development of the Organization of Anglo-American Trade, 1800–50* (New Haven: Yale University Press, 1925).

Catterall, Ralph C. H., *The Second Bank of the United States* (Chicago: University of Chicago Press, 1902).

Chambers, William Nisbet, *Old Bullion Benton, Senator from the New West* (Boston: Little, Brown, 1956).

Chandler, Lester V., *The Economics of Money and Banking*. 4th ed. (New York: Harper and Row, 1964).

Clapham, Sir John, *The Bank of England* (Cambridge, England: Cambridge University Press, 1944).

Cole, Arthur Harrison, *Wholesale Commodity Prices in the United States, 1700–1861*. 2 vols. (Cambridge: Harvard University Press, 1938).

Conrad, Alfred H., and John R. Meyer, *The Economics of Slavery* (Chicago: Aldine, 1964).

Davis, Lance E., and Jonathan R. T. Hughes, "A Dollar-Sterling Exchange, 1803–1895," *Economic History Review,* Second Series, XIII (August, 1960), 52–78.

Davis, Lance E., and John Legler, "The Government in the American Economy, 1815–1902: A Quantitative Study," *Journal of Economic History,* XXVI (December, 1966), 514–52.

Davis, Lance E., and H. Louis Stettler, III, "The New England Textile Industry, 1825–60: Trends and Fluctuations," in *Output, Employment, and Productivity in the United States after 1800.* Studies in Income and Wealth, Vol. 30 (New York: Columbia University Press for the National Bureau of Economic Research, 1966).

Deane, Phyllis, "New Estimates of Gross National Product for the United Kingdom, 1830–1914," *Review of Income and Wealth,* XIV (June, 1968), 95–112.

Dillistin, William H., *Bank Note Reporters and Counterfeit Detectors, 1826–1866* (New York: American Numismatic Society, 1949).

Easterlin, Richard A., "Interregional Differences in Per Capita Income, Population, and Total Income, 1840–1950," in *Trends in the American Economy in the Nineteenth Century.* Studies in Income and Wealth, Vol. 24 (Princeton: Princeton University Press for the National Bureau of Economic Research, 1960).

Elliot, Jonathan, *The American Diplomatic Code.* 2 vols. (Washington, D. C., 1834).

Elliot, Jonathan, *The Funding System of the United States and Great Britain* (Washington, 1845). (Printed also as U. S. Congress, House Document 15, 28th Congress, 1st Session.)

Engerman, Stanley, and Robert W. Fogel, Data presented to the Purdue Conference, February, 1965.

Fairbank, John King, *Trade and Diplomacy on the China Coast* (Cambridge: Harvard University Press, 1953).

Fetter, Frank Whitson, *Development of British Monetary Orthodoxy, 1797–1875* (Cambridge: Harvard University Press, 1965).

Fish, Carl Russell, *The Rise of the Common Man, 1830–1850.* Vol. VI of Arthur M. Schlesinger and Dixon Ryan Fix (eds.), *A History of American Life* (New York: Macmillan, 1927).

Fishlow, Albert, "Antebellum Interregional Trade Reconsidered," *American Economic Review, Papers and Proceedings,* LIV (May, 1964), 352–64.

Foreman, Grant, *Indian Removal: The Emigration of the Five Civ-*

ilized Tribes of Indians (Norman, Okla.: University of Oklahoma Press, 1932)

Friedman, Milton, and Anna Jacobson Schwartz, *A Monetary History of the United States, 1867–1960* (Princeton: Princeton University Press, 1963).

Gallatin, Albert, *Suggestions on the Banks and Currency of the Several States, in Reference Principally to the Suspension of Specie Payments* (New York, 1841).

Gallman, Robert E., "A Note on the Patent Office Crop Estimates, 1841–1848," *Journal of Economic History,* XXIII (June, 1963), 185–95.

Gallman, Robert E., "Gross National Product in the United States, 1834–1909," in *Output, Employment, and Productivity in the United States after 1800.* Studies in Income and Wealth, Vol. 30 (New York: Columbia University Press for the National Bureau of Economic Research, 1966).

Gatell, Frank Otto, "Sober Second Thoughts on Van Buren, the Albany Regency, and the Wall Street Conspiracy," *Journal of American History,* LIII (June, 1966), 19–40.

Gottlieb, Manuel, *Estimates of Residential Building, 1840–1939,* National Bureau of Economic Research Technical Paper 17 (New York: National Bureau of Economic Research, 1964).

Gouge, William M., *An Inquiry into the Principles of the American Banking System* (Philadelphia, 1833).

Govan, Thomas Payne, *Nicholas Biddle: Nationalist and Public Banker, 1786–1844* (Chicago: University of Chicago Press, 1959).

Gray, Lewis Cecil, *History of Agriculture in the Southern United States* (Washington: The Carnegie Institution, 1933).

Hall, James, *The West; Its Commerce and Navigation* (Cincinnati, 1848).

Hammond, Bray, *Banks and Politics in America, from the Revolution to the Civil War* (Princeton: Princeton University Press, 1957).

Handlin, Oscar and Mary Flug, *Commonwealth; A Study of the Role of Government in the American Economy: Massachusetts, 1774–1861* (New York: New York University Press, 1947).

Heath, Milton, *Constructive Liberalism; The Role of the State in Economic Development in Georgia to 1860* (Cambridge: Harvard University Press, 1954).

Hidy, Ralph W., *The House of Baring in American Trade and Finance* (Cambridge: Harvard University Press, 1949).

Hill, Hamilton A., *Memoir of Abbot Lawrence* (Cambridge, 1884).

Hofstadter, Richard, *The American Political Tradition* (New York: Knopf, 1948). (Page references from the Vintage edition.)

Homer, Sidney, *A History of Interest Rates* (New Brunswick, N. J.: Rutgers University Press, 1963).

Hughes, J. R. T., and Nathan Rosenberg, "The United States Business Cycle Before 1860: Some Problems of Interpretation," *Economic History Review,* Second Series, XV (1963), 476–93.

Hugins, Walter, *Jacksonian Democracy and the Working Class* (Stanford: Stanford University Press, 1960).

Imlah, Albert H., *Economic Elements in the Pax Britannica* (Cambridge: Harvard University Press, 1958).

Jackson, Andrew, "Veto Message," July 10, 1832, in James D. Richardson, *Message and Papers of the Presidents, 1789–1897.* 10 vols. (Washington, 1898–99), II, 576–91.

Jenks, Leland H., *The Migration of British Capital to 1875* (New York: Alfred A. Knopf, 1927).

Laughlin, J. Lawrence, *The History of Bimetallism in the United States,* 4th ed. (New York, 1897).

Lebergott, Stanley, *Manpower in Economic Growth: The American Record since 1800* (New York: McGraw-Hill, 1964).

Lewis, J. Parry, *Building Cycles and Britain's Growth* (New York: St. Martin's Press, 1965).

Macesich, George, "Sources of Monetary Disturbances in the U. S., 1834–1845," *Journal of Economic History,* XX (September, 1960), 407–34.

Macesich, George, "International Trade and United States Economic Development Revisited," *Journal of Economic History,* XXI (September, 1961), 384–85.

Marshall, Lynn L., "The Authorship of Jackson's Bank Veto Message," *Journal of American History,* L (December, 1963), 466–77.

Martin, R. Montgomery, *China: Political, Commercial, and Social; in an Official Report to Her Majesty's Government* (London, 1847).

Matthews, R. C. O., *A Study in Trade-Cycle History: Economic Fluctuations in Great Britain, 1833–1842* (Cambridge, England: Cambridge University Press, 1954).

McCormick, Richard P., *The Second American Party System: Party Formulation in the Jacksonian Era* (Chapel Hill: University of North Carolina Press, 1966).

McGouldrick, Paul F., *New England Textiles in the Nineteenth Century: Profits and Investment* (Cambridge: Harvard University Press, 1968).

McGrane, Reginald Charles, *The Panic of 1837* (Chicago: University of Chicago Press, 1924).

McLendon, S. G., *History of the Public Domain of Georgia* (Atlanta: Foote & Davies, 1924).

Meerman, Jacob P., "The Climax of the Bank War: Biddle's Contraction, 1833–34," *Journal of Political Economy*, LXXI (August, 1963), 378–88.

Meyers, Marvin, *The Jacksonian Persuasion* (Stanford: Stanford University Press, 1960).

Mitchell, B. R., and Phyllis Deane, *Abstract of British Historical Statistics* (Cambridge, England: Cambridge University Press, 1962).

Morison, Samuel Eliot, *The Maritime History of Massachusetts, 1783–1860* (Boston: Houghton Mifflin, Sentry Edition, 1961).

Morison, Samuel Eliot, and Henry Steele Commager, *The Growth of the American Republic*, 5th ed. (New York: Oxford University Press, 1962).

Myers, Margaret G., *The New York Money Market*. 2 vols. (New York: Columbia University Press, 1931).

Niles' Weekly Register (Baltimore, 1811–49).

North, Douglass C., "The United States Balance of Payments, 1790–1860," in *Trends in the American Economy in the Nineteenth Century*. Studies in Income and Wealth, Vol. 24 (Princeton: Princeton University Press for the National Bureau of Economic Research, 1960).

North, Douglass C., *The Economic Growth of the United States, 1790–1860* (New York: Norton, 1966).

North, Douglass C., *Growth and Welfare in the American Past* (Englewood Cliffs: Prentice-Hall, 1966).

Nussbaum, Arthur, *A History of the Dollar* (New York: Columbia University Press, 1957).

O'Leary, Paul M., "The Coinage Legislation of 1834," *Journal of Political Economy*, XLV (February, 1937), 80–94.

Palmer, J. Horsley, *The Causes and Consequences of the Pressure upon the Money Market* (London, 1837).

Potter, J., "Atlantic Economy, 1815–60: The U. S. A. and the Industrial Revolution in Britain," in L. S. Pressnell (ed.), *Studies in the Industrial Revolution* (London: University of London Press, 1960).

Primack, Martin, "Land Clearing Under Nineteenth-Century Techniques. Some Preliminary Calculations," *Journal of Economic History*, XXII (December, 1962), 484–97.

Ratchford, B. U., *American State Debts* (Durham, N. C.: Duke University Press, 1941).

Redlich, Fritz, *The Molding of American Banking: Men and Ideas* (New York: Hafner Publishing Co., 1951).

Redlich, Fritz, and Webster M. Christman, "Early Checks and an Example of Their Use," *Business History Review*, XLI (Autumn, 1967), 285–302.

Remini, Robert V., *Andrew Jackson and the Bank War* (New York: Norton, 1967).

Rezneck, Samuel, "Social History of an American Depression, 1837–1843," *American Historical Review*, XL (July, 1935), 662–87.

Scheiber, Harry N., "The Pet Banks in Jacksonian Politics and Finance, 1833–41," *Journal of Economic History*, XXIII (June, 1963), 196–214.

Schlesinger, Arthur M., Jr., *The Age of Jackson* (Boston: Little Brown, 1945).

Schur, Leon M., "The Second Bank of the United States and the Inflation after the War of 1812," *Journal of Political Economy* LXVIII (April, 1960), 118–34.

Schwartz, Anna Jacobson, "Pennsylvania and New York Banking Statistics," Unpublished paper for the National Bureau of Economic Research.

Smith, Walter Buckingham, *Economic Aspects of the Second Bank of the United States* (Cambridge: Harvard University Press, 1953).

Smith, Walter Buckingham, and Arthur Harrison Cole, *Fluctuations in American Business, 1790–1860* (Cambridge: Harvard University Press, 1935).

Sumner, William Graham, *A History of Banking in the United States* (New York, 1896).

Swisher, Carl Brent, *Roger B. Taney* (New York: Macmillan, 1935).

Taus, Esther Rogoff, *Central Banking Functions of the United States Treasury, 1789–1941* (New York: Columbia University Press, 1943).

Taylor, George Rogers, *The Transportation Revolution* (New York: Holt, Rinehart and Winston, 1951).

Temin, Peter, *Iron and Steel in Nineteenth-Century America: An Economic Inquiry* (Cambridge: M.I.T. Press, 1964).

Temin, Peter, "The Causes of Cotton-Price Fluctuations in the 1830's," *Review of Economics and Statistics*, XLIX (Nov., 1967), 463–470.

Thistlethwaithe, Frank, *The Great Experiment* (Cambridge, England: Cambridge University Press, 1955).

Timberlake, Richard H., Jr., "The Specie Circular and the Distribution of the Surplus," *Journal of Political Economy*, LXVIII (April, 1960), 109–17.

Timberlake, Richard H., Jr., "The Specie Standard and Central Banking in the United States before 1860," *Journal of Economic History*, XXI (September, 1961), 318–41.

Timberlake, Richard H., Jr., "The Specie Circular and Sales of Public Lands: A Comment," *Journal of Economic History*, XXV (September, 1965), 414–16.

Tooke, Thomas, *A History of Prices and of the State of the Circulation, from 1793 to 1856.* 6 vols. (London, 1838–57).

Towne, Marvin W., and Wayne D. Rasmussen, "Farm Gross Product and Gross Investment in the Nineteenth Century," in *Trends in the American Economy in the Nineteenth Century.* Studies in Income and Wealth, Vol. 24 (Princeton: Princeton University Press for the National Bureau of Economic Research, 1960).

U. S. Bureau of the Census, *Historical Statistics of the United States, Colonial Times to 1957* (Washington, D. C., 1960).

U. S. Comptroller of the Currency, *Report,* 1896.

U. S. Congress, House Document 30, 25th Congress, 1st Session (1837).

U. S. Congress, House Document 111, 26th Congress, 2nd Session (1841).

U. S. Congress, House Document 68, 31st Congress, 1st Session (1850).

U. S. Congress, House Report 460, 22nd Congress, 1st Session (1832).

U. S. Congress, Senate Document 356, 24th Congress, 1st Session (1836).

U. S. Congress, Senate Document 29, 24th Congress, 2nd Session (1836).

U. S. Congress, Senate Document 128, 25th Congress, 2nd Session (1838).

U. S. Congress, Senate Document 351, 25th Congress, 2nd Session (1838).

U. S. Department of Agriculture, Division of Statistics, *Miscellaneous Series Bulletin 9.* "Production and Price of Cotton for One Hundred Years," by James L. Watkins (Washington, 1895).

U. S. Department of Agriculture, Bureau of Statistics, *Circular 32,* "Cotton Crop of the United States, 1790–1911" (Washington, 1912).

U. S. Treasury Department, *Annual Reports on Commerce and Navigation*. Printed as House Executive Documents.

U. S. Treasury, *Reports of the Secretary of the Treasury of the United States*. 5 vols. (Washington, 1837, 1851).

Van Buren, Martin, "Autobiography," *Annual Report of the American Historical Association for 1918* (Washington: Government Printing Office, 1920).

Van Deusen, Glyndon G., *The Jacksonian Era: 1828–1848* (New York: Harper & Row, 1959).

Van Every, Dale, *Disinherited: The Lost Birthright of the American Indian* (New York: Morrow, 1966).

Van Fenstermaker, J., *The Development of American Commercial Banking, 1782–1837* (Kent, Ohio: Kent State University, 1965).

Walker, Amasa, *The Science of Wealth* (Boston, 1866).

Wellington, Raynor G., *The Political and Sectional Influence of the Public Lands, 1828–42* (Cambridge: Riverside Press, 1914).

Wilburn, Jean Alexander, *Biddle's Bank: The Crucial Years* (New York: Columbia University Press, 1967).

Williams, T. H., R. N. Current and F. Freidel, *A History of the United States* (New York: Knopf, 1959).

Williamson, Jeffrey G., "International Trade and United States Economic Development: 1827–1843," *Journal of Economic History*, XXI (September, 1961), 372–83.

Williamson, Jeffrey G., *American Growth and the Balance of Payments, 1820–1913: A Study of the Long Swing* (Chapel Hill: University of North Carolina Press, 1964).

Wiltse, Charles M., *John C. Calhoun, Nullifier, 1829–39* (Indianapolis: Bobbs-Merrill, 1949).

Young, Mary E., "Indian Removal and Land Allotment: The Civilized Tribes and Jacksonian Justice," *American Historical Review*, LXIV (October, 1958), 31–45.

Zevin, Robert B., "The Growth of Cotton Textile Production After 1815," forthcoming.

Index